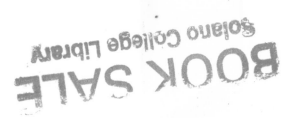
CT
3202   Harms, Valerie
H37
          Stars in my sky

DATE DUE

4/7			

50282

Maria Montessori
Anaïs Nin
Frances Steloff

Stars In My Sky
by
Valerie Harms

Order from:
Walker & Company
720 Fifth Avenue
New York, New York, 10019

ACKNOWLEDGMENTS

Thanks are gratefully extended to the following institutions, publishers, and individuals for material used in these pages:

To the Montessori Studies Center for the diagram of Prepared Paths to Culture;

To Holt, Rinehart and Winston, Inc., for quotations from **The Absorbent Mind** by Maria Montessori;

To Schocken Books, Inc., for quotations from Maria Montessori's **Spontaneous Activity in Education, Secret of Childhood, From Childhood to Adolescence;**

To Fides Publishers, Inc., for quotations from **Secret of Childhood** by Maria Montessori;

To the Association Montessori Internationale for quotations from the **Montessori Centenary Anthology;**

To Frances Steloff for quotations from her memoirs;

To Swallow Press, Inc., and Gunther Stuhlmann for quotations from **House of Incest** by Anais Nin;

To Harcourt Brace Jovanovich, Inc., for quotations from the **Diary of Anais Nin;**

To the Macmillan Publishing Company, Inc., for quotations from **Novel of the Future** by Anais Nin;

To Dr. Ira Progoff for the quotation from **At a Journal Workshop;**

To United Press International for the photograph of Maria Montessori;

To Arnold Eagle Productions for the photograph of Frances Steloff;

To Margo Moore for the photograph of Anais Nin;

To Sas Colby for cover design;

And to Moira Collins for calligraphy.

Preface

From a definition of wisdom figures in
At a Journal Workshop:

**They are persons of profound importance
to us in specific relation to our inner experience
and to the enlargement of our consciousness.**

**Their principal characteristic is that they are
individuals who represent wisdom to us with
respect to some particular area of our lives
and who, at least in our perception of them,
embody a capacity of deep and direct knowing.**

Dr. Ira Progoff

This is a biographical book about Maria Montessori, Anais Nin,
Frances Steloff — and me. It is based on years of acquaintance and
long preoccupation with the work of these women, as well as personal friendship with Anais Nin and Frances Steloff. (Maria Montessori
died when I was 12 years old). In my portraits of these women I
view the content of their work with a psychological eye.

This book is not a critical evaluation of these women's roles in
history, although it delves into the pioneering contributions made by
the women. I have tried to present the inner essence of each woman
and show how that essence played a meaningful role in my life. At
different periods of my life each one was like a numinous, twinkling
star that guided me. I was hitched to each woman by inner cords;
writing these portraits has been an exploration of this mysterious
form of energy. This book, thus, can be seen as only part of the
women's multi-faceted reality, but my subjective approach should
touch upon universal meanings. Anais Nin expressed this hope in
saying, **The personal life deeply lived expands into truths beyond
itself.**

The women are similar in many ways. They are international figures both by heritage and in the scope of their work. Maria Montessori developed an educational theory that she translated into action in schools that were established in countries all over the world. Anais Nin is the author of numerous literary works, including novels, stories, criticism, and six volumes of **The Diary of Anais Nin.** Born in France, living in Cuba for a time and much longer in America, this writer absorbed the special qualities of French, Spanish, and English. Although her books were originally published in English, they have been translated into every major language. Frances Steloff is a first-generation American born of Russian parents. She opened the unique Gotham Book Mart in New York City and drew together authors and readers around the globe.

Furthermore, each woman had a sense of destiny unfolding in her life and had the courage to face the unknown with total dedication. Each in her own way blended practicality with mysticism. Each in her separate field was aware of the powers of the unconscious. Montessori was the first philosopher to focus on the psychic evolutional growth of the child and to use it in the construction of a new world. Nin in her writing dwelled intensively on the psychological constellations of men and women and warned that psychic integration was a personal struggle absolutely essential to save the world from human destruction. And for Steloff her daily obstacles in work at the Gotham Book Mart became the substance and discipline of her spiritual transformation. Morally and socially all the women persevered in their diverse efforts to achieve harmony in the world.

The real underlying similarity of the women though remains that they served as wisdom figures, soul mothers, carriers of light and wisdom to me. They sensitized me to areas of knowledge, both inner and outer, lunar and solar, for which I am grateful. I hope that other people may be encouraged by this book to have inner dialogues with their soul stars.

Stars In My Sky

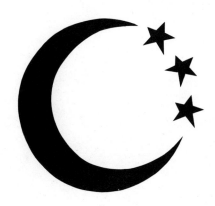

Maria Montessori

Children of the Cosmos

Most people, if they have heard of Montessori, think of schools for toddlers. The fact is Montessori was far more than an early childhood educator. She was also a doctor and most importantly a social philosopher, passionately intent on the transformation of society. Montessori felt that the social organization of the world was bent on destruction when it could be positively regenerating humanity and the natural resources. Today the mass of people generally are aware of what Montessori foresaw fifty years ago. Witness a recent *New York Times* editorial by Stephen Spender:

> **It seems quite probable that by the end of the century an overpopulated, polluted, fragmented world will collapse into wars and revolutions, perhaps the end of most human life. The ultimate reasons for the collapse will lie in the failure of multiple human natures to become one humanity capable of adapting itself to conditions which human beings, with their science and technology, have themselves produced.**

Montessori devoted herself to the cause of world construction. She pondered humanity to find out what characteristics could be turned to the world's advantage and how the present course of events could be averted. Politicians were of no use; they could only cope with the symptoms of failure and not the causes. Adults seemed confined by innate egocentricity to their separate bodies, unable to get past the limits of their separate families, nations, races, and creeds. She found the answer in the human child. She spent an active, learned, innovative life revealing the qualities of children in relation to the future of the world. However, rather than theorize on her profound insights, she found it more useful to observe children constantly and create potential-releasing environments for them. She clung tenaciously to the intangible, but powerful, human spirit.

Observing the spirit of a child is very hard to do. Since the birth of my first child 12 years ago, I have been ridding myself of cultural misconceptions, as I grow more influenced by the ideas of Maria Montessori. I have read the opinions of many educators and philosophers and found that although their purposes were admirable, their theories lasted only as long as sugar-coated cereal; whereas the work of Montessori was constantly fertilizing and enriching me. She had an awesome respect for the child and uniquely sensed the necessity to *see the child as she* was,* rather than as we subjectively would like her to be. Montessori advocated scientific contemplation of the child as a necessary act for the future.

I am sorry I never knew Montessori personally. She was born August 31, 1870 and died May 6, 1952. I was only 12 years old then and preoccupied with the forces acting on me as I grew up myself rather than seeing them as part of a universal happening. But I have been drawn to Montessori for many years for complex reasons. First of all, I am a mother concerned with the raising of human children. Second, as a woman she was a pioneer in her career development. She was the first woman doctor in Italy and then the constructor of the world's most compassionate and adaptable educational system. In international conferences she also trained teachers in the subtle approach required to make the system

---

*Throughout this essay I have elected to use the word "she" instead of "he", and "her" instead of "his", whenever people or humanity as a whole is implied. The words "she" and "he" contain within themselves the letters of "he", but "he" and "him" do not contain *she.* Thus, "she" seems more inclusive. Readers, I hope, will find this a provocative experience, perhaps just because the norm is gone against. I have not, however, altered words in quotations from Montessori.

work, and through lectures and the writing of numerous books she sought to make parents of the world and governments understand the importance of children. She related education to the welfare of society as a whole, going so far as to organize a political party for children. And she was a spiritual thinker whose vision of peace and life in the cosmos was admired by her contemporaries, including philosophers like Gandhi, Bertrand Russell, Sigmund and Anna Freud. Although Montessori's ideas became a movement, in spite of her, she encountered major resistance in people who were not ready for her. Now almost a quarter of a century after her death, world thinkers such as Buckminster Fuller and Bruno Bettleheim are echoing what she said.

Keenly felt personal need led me to Montessori. My three-year-old daughter had been spending her mornings at "Aunt Julie's Play School", essentially a baby-sitting program where children colored and painted and watched television. I was discouraged by its frivolity, yet saw nothing for pre-schoolers, and was glad at least that my daughter had the company of other youngsters. One day I heard about the Child's Work Center, a school *based on the Montessori Method.* It sounded odd, but I investigated it. On closed circuit t.v. I watched a class of approximately 30 children. The children were engaged in separate activities. One girl arranged flowers in a vase; a boy polished shoes. Another girl put letters back into a compartmentalized box, having finished spelling out words with them. No teacher apparently hovered nearby directing them. The children seemed to know exactly what they were doing and to be enjoying it. I was amazed at the intellectual accomplishment and the opportunity for the children to do basic acts of living so graciously. I swiftly endeavored to have my daughter included in the group. I knew I didn't want my daughter to spend another minute in the suffocating atmosphere at Aunt Julie's.

Since then both my children have been exposed to only a Montessori environment. My daughter, at 12, has gone as far as she can in her school, as presently there are no institutions for the teenager in this country. My son began Montessori school when he was 2½. At home my husband and I are earnest practitioners and have encountered our own strengths and weaknesses in the process (child-raising being a most demanding adventure in inner discipline). In my absorption I read and reread Montessori's books, plus many

articles written about her work. I have talked to dozens of teachers,
visited schools, and attended conferences. For several years I served
on the board of my children's school and concerned myself with
the administration of the school, a very unsatisfying experience
because the adults fought and were unable to work in association
as the children did. Again and again I felt that there was so much
children could teach us, and I would go to Montessori to point the
way.

Maria Montessori was born and raised in Italy. She was imbued
with that country's spirit of Catholicism and joy in children. She
confronted Italian patriarchal attitudes at several points in her life
with an early sense of self-worth. When she was 16 years old, she
entered technical school in order to become an engineer. She and
the only other female student in the school were kept inside during
recess to avoid harassment by the male students. After technical
school, she decided to study medicine rather than engineering,
which infuriated her father. She sought permission from the head
of the Board of Education but was refused. She persevered and
won acceptance, becoming estranged from her father in the process.
Eventually when Maria Montessori became Italy's first woman doctor, the honor won her father back. She also never married but
raised her own child and gave speeches, such as at the International
Congress for Women's Rights on behalf of equal pay for men and
women. Although little is published about her private life, her
independence and self-possession declare themselves in her acts, as
if preparing her early for larger battlefields.

An event occurred at medical school that set Montessori on
the path toward the study of the child. She says she was in a state
of dejection. The other medical students, all men, were hostile to
her. Because she was a woman, she was not allowed to study the
anatomy of the body with them but had to spend long hours alone
with the corpses. Dissection depressed her, one day so horribly that
she left the room, determined to find a solution to her problems.
While she was walking on the street, she passed a shabbily dressed
woman with a child of about two years. The woman begged for
money in a whining tone. Her little child, quite unconcerned, sat
on the ground playing with a short red string. The child was intently
absorbed in the little string and appeared serenely happy. A flash of
significance overcame Montessori, an inner awareness that enabled

her to go back to the dissection room and finish her medical studies purposefully. The event crystallized in her mind things that had been brewing unconsciously during the years of her studies. Just as Newton, having mulled the problem of gravity for a long time, grasped its essence when the apple fell on his head, so at last after Montessori's mental tussling came a moment when the answer was partially revealed. For Montessori it was the essence of childhood. Destiny's seed was born.

This seed led the young Dr. Montessori to practice her medical work on children. Her first duties were in a hospital, dealing with nervous and mental cases, including mentally defective children. These children Montessori nurtured so well that they passed examinations given to normal children. This made Montessori question what was wrong with society's cultivation of normal children.

Montessori approached this question from her scientific and medical background. For her the real study was life, and she always talked about her ideas and materials in terms of how they were a **help to life.** She had thoroughly assimilated the beginnings of life in studying the structure of the cell and the evolution of plants, animals, and humans according to organic dynamic principles of growth. Confining her thoughts to people, she saw childhood as the cell foreshadowing the person-to-be. In childhood was a nucleus of unrevealed potentialities and élan vital, an energy that she began to see as important to the world as the discovery of the atom. As constructive as the bomb would be destructive.

While Montessori the scientist mulled over the chemical, physical, biological, geographical side of things and Montessori the medical doctor examined growing bodies under the varying influences of light, air, nutrition and exercise, her spirit was also at work. She gave her spirit time. One example occurred when she was working at an institute in Rome for training teachers of mentally defective children and studying the work of Itard and Séguin. Feeling the need for meditation, she withdrew from active work to study them more thoroughly. She translated and by hand copied the writings of these men from beginning to end, making books such as Benedictine monks used to do before the diffusion of printing. She wanted to fully weigh each word.

By the time Montessori was 37 years old, in addition to practicing medicine, she had spent 16 years lecturing in anthropology at universities and colleges and written a book entitled **Pedagogical Anthropology.** She possessed an abundance of physical and intellectual grace. Her son, Mario, lived with her, although there had been some difficulties over his custody. (This son later would devote his life to his mother's work, becoming after her death the leader of The Association Montessori Internationale and a widely respected educator.) An opportunity now presented itself to Montessori; in it she recognized her longing for this destiny, and readily seized it.

The year was 1907. The city of Rome had demolished a disgusting slum area and erected new housing in its place. Within the housing area a place was set aside for the children of the mothers who worked. The children's area was bare and totally under the charge of its director, the position which Montessori assumed as a challenge. She dubbed the area *Casa dei Bambini,* meaning Children's House. And here in the empty room in a ghetto Montessori found the freedom to express the philosophical flame burning in her heart and mind.

The day of the housing's dedication was January 6th, for Christians *Epiphany* or the day of the Feast of the Children, which commemorated the time when the three Kings arrived before the Christ Child bearing gifts. Montessori said that as she spoke about the Casa dei Bambini a vision came to her, vividly depicting a future day when people would come from all over the world to see the poor children of the Casa. And it happened. Very soon this modern Pilgrim beginning with bereft children and no provisions or food, did see modern kings in the clothes of world leaders and educators visit that place and marvel. But for the present she had only her faith in the children's promise.

About her experience she said in retrospect: **I set to work, like a peasant woman who, having set aside a good store of seed corn, has found a fertile field in which she may freely sow it. But I was wrong. I had hardly turned over the clods of my field when I found** *gold* **instead of wheat.** Her methods were so successful that other schools sprang up in Africa, India, the Americas, all of Europe. She published **The Montessori Method** and in 1912 went on a lecture tour in the U.S., at which time Alexander Graham Bell started the first Montessori Association here and the Governor of Rhode Island announced that her *method* was to be introduced in all public schools.

During the years 1916-18 Montessori divided her time between pedagogical courses given in California and Spain. Henceforth her years would be devoted to research, lectures, training courses, and the writing of 13 more books. The teacher training courses were given to people from all over the world in centers in England, Austria, Germany, Holland, and Italy. Schools and associations were formed continuously. Jean Piaget became president of the Swiss Montessori Society. In 1929 The Association Montessori Internationale was founded in Denmark; it is now the publishing house of *Communications,* the central organ of Montessori activities.

The war years and post-war reaction were disastrous for Montessori. In Italy she was ostracized because she opposed Fascism and World War II. Her books and effigy were burned publicly. During Spain's Civil War she was forced to leave that country. However, forced departures from one country led her to establish schools in others, which caused her work to spread. From Spain she went to the Netherlands; from Italy she resided in India, becoming well received and established there. She began to think of herself as a citizen of the world, realizing profoundly how dangerous nationalism was.

Although eventually Montessori would be reinstated with honor by the Italian government and even eulogized by UNESCO in 1950 for being a symbol of peace, her work suffered in this country because of post-war attitudes. For one thing, she seemed too spiritual at a time when America was becoming most materialistic due to its new prosperity. (India, by significant contrast, had been a most receptive climate.) Many people today still erroneously think a Montessori school means a Catholic one. She faced criticism for being too rigid as well, whereas before the war when highly disciplined classroom education was the mode, she was considered too experimental. But in the late 1940's the progressive, *activity* oriented educators looked down on her for not permitting total freedom to the children, a freedom which she scorned as being *license.* Indirectly her treatment of art hurt her cause too, for the popular mind was beginning to worship the idea of *creativity* which developed into the most random of activities, producing such dismal classroom projects as entire classes drawing pussywillows in the spring, pumpkins in the fall, etc. Also, as a woman she did not have the support or attention that the public media easily afforded men, contemporaries such as John Dewey and Piaget or even the younger men, Jerome Bruner and Bruno Bettleheim. Even now mothers who have spent more hours with children than many educators or doctors are not sought for their experiential insights into child behavior; we read instead the opinions of John Holt, George Dennison, and Dr. Salk. Possibly the time has come for Montessori to be truly appreciated, for now some patriarchal attitudes are less stringent and the totally free schools have not succeeded. An example of change can be seen in California's recent decision to divert funds for learning to early childhood programs rather than to the colleges — a recognition of the lasting importance of the formative years.

As an educator, Montessori blends the seemingly opposite twins, science and religion. The salient features of her theory, involving the human organism, the psychic embryo, absorbent mind, cultural adaptation and cosmic evolution compose a kind of spiritual biology. She does not see education as just a portion of life but as a process going on the full length of life, concerned with the development of a passionate soul as well as an intellectual mind. For Montessori the goal of education is to enable the individual to experience joy and easy adaptation to the cultural environment. Because she was convinced that children contained the key to the successful evolution of humanity, she emphasized how important it was for the future to harmonize the child's physical growth with absorption of cultural facts.

The golden key (the **secret of childhood** as Montessori called it), is the child's psychic energy. Psychic energy does not refer here to ESP, the power of mind over matter, healing, mediumship, or reincarnation, although these can be regarded as aspects of mental energy. Rather, Montessori meant the fusing of body and mind by the spirit that vitally animates human beings. All forms of nature are so inhabited, which we realize when we open ourselves to their reality. This energy is a supra-conscious force that makes activity easy and elevating when it is worked with or fatiguing and poor when it is gone against. Montessori made elaborate comparisons between human cells and those of plants and animals, focusing on the cell's capacity to separate into parts and perform different functions, all of which contribute to the whole. Each part has its own time-table which also governs instincts. For instance, a bird will not have the instinct to fly until some time after it has been hatched. Hidden in the embryo is the code for growth. She writes:

Just as every fertilized cell contains within itself the plan of the whole organism, so the body of a new-born creature, no matter to what species it may belong, has within itself psychic instincts which will enable it to adjust to its surroundings. (Secret of Childhood)

The psychic instincts of the species are common to all, no matter what race or origin. Thus, all children talk, walk, change teeth around the same age, as well as display other characteristics in common which Montessori defined at length in her scheme of the stages of human growth.

The human embryo is not a helpless, stupid creature but a nucleus of potentialities to be developed according to her physical interaction in the world-environment, her intelligence, and the driving force of her unconscious. The wonderful quality of the child's mind is that it is absorbent. It learns effortlessly and is totally sensitive to the present moment and environment, all of which is assimilated by the unconscious. This absorbent mind enables children to learn their native language with none of the struggle encountered by adults learning a language. The child's mode is easy when the sensitivity exists. When the special sensitivity departs, learning becomes difficult. An example is the case of a child who does not hear any language at all during the period of acoustic sensitivity. Such a child becomes a deaf mute, even though her hearing is fine. Montessori carefully analyzed these sensitive periods in the growth of children. She saw a close relationship between the person and things of the culture so that when sensitivity — or enthusiasm — exists, the child's mind is readily able to absorb the subject. Thus, adults should create environments for children where these sensitivities can freely emerge and be fulfilled by the materials available. Because Montessori believed every child represents a step in the evolution of humanity. she emphasized that guidance shift from the adult to the inner directives of the child, and the adult become disciplined in observation. For the long infancy of human beings is intended to give the child time to equip herself to take part in the culture in a responsible, preserving way, and during this period the child needs proper assistance. Montessori wrote:

Children take from the environment language, religion, customs and the peculiarities not only of the race, not only of the nation, but even of a special district in which they develop . . . Childhood constructs with what it finds. If the material is poor, the construction is also poor.

In her theory of education Montessori was one of the first to be influenced by research on the unconscious functioning of the mind. She wrote about the use of it in the learning process, how it was fundamental to the accumulation of facts, ideas, sensations. The unconscious for her was a vast storehouse of knowledge, built up by the child's interaction with the environment. The child explores her world with her senses and through manipulation of concrete objects receives innumerable impressions for future synthesis. The child's opportunities for meaningful activity (termed *work* by Montessori) are therefore crucial in the development of the child's unconscious.

To Montessori allowing the unconscious the freedom to associate ideas spontaneously was to make positive use of it; suppressing or ignoring it was to bring forth its negative aspects. Repression, caused by fear of the dark unknown, arouses epidemics of psychological illness in people, because the unconscious is too strong to be contained by the human will. War, she maintained, was a mass cancerous infection of the unconscious, with greater power to destroy the earth and humanity than the natural holocausts of volcanoes and hurricanes. Montessori ardently wished to eliminate fear in the human mind and restore psychological health. For her education concerned the person's process of psychological integration as well as individuation.

Beyond seeing the biological and psychological aspects of the human being in relation to its role on earth, Montessori had a metaphysical vision of the cosmos. In this view the mind and body of humans, the plants, fish, animals, minerals, all forms of existence belong to One Moving Principle (Cosmic Mind, Supraconscious, God). In essence the 32 elements forming the multiplicity of things in this world are energy nuclei. Atoms are like minute solar systems. The apparently immobile stone hides an intense life. The molecules of a diamond oscillate 19,000 billion times per second. Solid matter is really full of empty spaces in which a great deal of activity is going on. The elements of all matter are centers of force or series of waves, dancing perpetually in dizzying rhythms. The whole universe from the atom to the star is literally suspended in this intensely moving reality. The only substantial reality is change.

Human children, partaking of this cosmic reality, are thus moving energy patterns. Like all forms of existence, they have a significant role to play in the ecological chain, one that is based on cooperation with the elements of the universe. As doctor, anthropologist, zoologist, and biologist, Montessori was thoroughly aware of the physical laws governing the evolution of life in the universe and saw closely united the cosmic function of the human being. In her method of education she emphasized providing the child with the freedom and independence essential to growth but channeling her activity toward a knowing, harmonious relationship with the culture.

In Montessori's plan for Cosmic Education she shows how all life, including humanity, serves the universe. This is the cosmic task of all. The human being is the cosmos' agent for service and change and affects life for generations. Montessori would inspire children with extended narratives that detailed the unity of the world. She taught how useful all people in the past have been in making possible life as we know it today. The people who grew food, sold it, made clothes and furniture have all been dependent on each other's work. She created a reverence for people and their achievements in the past. History is taught in terms of the earth and people rather than changes wrought through warfare.

In her cosmic drama she would show how natural functions, such as breathing, are designed to serve the world. Human breathing is essential to the life of plants: the plants take in carbon dioxide and give us back oxygen. Humans are parasites on the earth's minerals, animals, and vegetables in filling their needs to eat, be clothed and sheltered. As an example of how all created things are dependent on each other in a complex, organized, unconscious way, the sun melts ice on top of the mountains forming rivers, lakes, and oceans which nourish all life. The butterfly in feeding itself takes nectar from a flower and serves the flower by fertilizing it. Even carnivorous feeding on other animals keeps the species fitter and more alert. She said one of nature's laws is that when serving the world, a being is also serving itself; there is an egoism that works for others. She felt that in society too many people have weak wills and cannot apply themselves to the cosmic purpose. They are caught like cogs in machines, slaves to another's charisma. But our duty is to breathe and feed ourselves, love one another, raise the standard of culture, and create new instruments which transform and utilize the energies of nature. In this perspective on humanity, the goal of earning money and achieving success is obviously a petty individual concern, one that narrows drastically the vision of anyone who attempts to live by it or impose it as a goal on children.

To children's delight she detailed the characteristics of humans and lower-order animals in order to better point out their specialized life-purposes. For instance, animals being incarnated in their bodies, are self-contained for survival (e.g., rodents with chiseling teeth, polar bears with thick fur); humans, not being confined to their bodies, use their brains and hands to make tools and weapons. Whereas animals will die if deprived of food sources, humans can plan for. their survival. Humans have stronger emotions. They can stand up to make their front limbs free. The fact that human children take longer to grow up than any animal baby is because their culture is more complex. Animals are satisfied when warm and fed, humans are by nature exploring and inquiring. Humans make rakes for themselves after the model of paws; they learn through trial and error that a straight stick works better than a crooked one, that it can be joined to others to make it longer, etc. Montessori showed that these differences indicate the direction in which nature has provided for humans to grow. Humans are intended to develop through movement, work, manipulation, and experience. They perfect themselves, increasing efficiency and refining the capacities of their movements, achieving ultimate self-control. Montessori always stressed how this form of self-mastery was the true liberation of the spirit, which permitted lasting satisfaction.

In Montessori's extensive teaching about the evolution of our cosmic *household,* humans come into the picture only recently. Because the universe has experimented with life for a long time before human beings, what possible future is intended for humanity, she asks? In **To Educate the Human Potential** there is a splendid example of how she presents the universe to children. In most traditional schools a young child is first exposed to things of her community, then of the state, then of the country, and finally of the world. Montessori began with the world, concentrating on the evolution of plants and animals, the glaciations which initiated geological eras, to the advent of humans. She writes lovingly of the sun and creation of the planet earth, creating a *drama of the oceans,* referring to fish as the *aristocracy* because of their high place in evolution. She describes how original sea material is modified over the centuries into beautiful marble and coral, how seas yield to growing lands, and continents dissolve into the sea. Water itself is a rhapsody of color and form, the wondrous source of life. She shows how nature prepared itself to receive animals, how conditions had to be made just right, and the wisdom and time behind the accomplishment of this. Life proceeded in eras and death has cosmic significance.

For example, the death of plants centuries ago resulted through fermentation and transformation in the storing up of coal, how vital to humanity. Earth wars — volcanoes — changed the face of the land. In Montessori's terms, when life shirked its duty of serving the earth, extinction resulted. Mankind now faces extinction because of violently neglecting its purpose and creating impossible conditions for survival.

In the study of earth's growth, she dwells on the creation of different civilizations from the earliest nomads and cultivators of the land, showing how the different conditions of continents such as Africa and North America presented distinct problems. Yet, through trade and warfare peoples mixed, provoking Montessori to compare nature to a chef, mixing her ingredients, bringing in strange and exotic essences, experimenting with what she was making. The effect of presenting material in this way has been to give children an identity in the universe, something so lacking among many of today's young. Children are awed and humbled by the enormity and flux of the universe.

Taught Cosmic Education, people are less likely to fall into the dangers of ignorance caused by over-specialization of knowledge. Such ignorance, for example businessmen not understanding chemistry, led to the pollution of waters and food. The cosmic view also provides a framework for sorting the confusing multiplicity of information that the media generates and gives exhausted individuals a unified picture of life in the universe. For in the cosmic plan we belong to the universe, and like our relatives, the plankton of the sea, our task and amazing significance is to live as fully as possible for the advantage of the species. As one manifestation of the total energy of the universe, humans are an experiment that is by no means eternal. More and more people recognize the necessity of the cosmic view, which can be seen in ecology groups, the food and fuel crises, the continued discussion of global or cosmic conscious-ness. *The New York Times* quoted recently Dr. Albert Einstein's view of cosmic unity among individual human beings:

> **A human being is a part of the whole, called by us**
> **Universe, a part limited in time and space. He**
> **experiences himself, his thoughts and feelings as some-**
> **thing separated from the rest — a kind of optical**
> **delusion of consciousness. This delusion is a kind of**
> **prison for us. Our task must be to free ourselves**
> **from this prison by widening our circle of compassion**
> **to embrace all living creatures and the whole nature**
> **in its beauty. Nobody is able to achieve this completely,**
> **but the striving for such achievement is in itself a part**
> **of the liberation and a foundation for inner security.**

But it is especially Buckminster Fuller whose voice most fami-liarly echoes Montessori's cosmic philosophy now. Buckminster Fuller describes how in the early age of human history parents were regarded as the authorities, life-supporters and source of all know-ledge. Then the automobile, radio and t.v. suddenly spread public information throughout the whole world instantly. Our parents became the authorities on very little anymore because culture and tradition changed radically, presenting problems on a global scale that were not solvable by usual methods of political leadership and wealth. He writes that humans living in this epoch have to use all their integrity, all their knowledge and technology to monitor the universe's problems. He bids goodbye to concepts of personal property and special advantage. Fuller, like Montessori, refers to the specialization of society's division of labor as an *abyss of ignorance.*

Fuller believes that the human metaphysical mind through intuition allows us to discover and use the eternal, weightless princi-ples governing the universe. He urges us to think in terms of whole systems, understanding the interconnectedness of things and using technology to enhance rather than violate natural balances. Further-more, in his **Education Automation** he expresses his conviction that education will become the major industry of the whole world with its emphasis on making the world's total resources serve 100% of humanity rather than the present rate of 43%. He urges that the focus be on what the universe is trying to do, why humans are a part of it, and how they can best function. This education necessarily goes on all one's life because of the fast and varied changes in the world.

As early as 1909, with the publication of **The Montessori Method,** Montessori clearly mapped out her educational theory that is designed to serve the future of the world. The keys to her method of education are perhaps even more vital today than when she launched them because people need an educational approach that will help them live in the environment before they cause their own extinction. So far adults have failed because they have tried to play God on earth. Montessori wrote:

> **How miserably our theories have guided us. War, famine, the destruction of natural resources are widespread. People themselves are out of joint; never has such dislocation, detachment from the earth been so prevalent, except for the new groups of ecologists in all professions of life. Our theories have come from the rationalizations of man. They have not sprung from the inner well-springs of beings in relation to the earth.**

Human beings have not been allowed to develop according to the genetic, biologic, and psychological imprint of their psyches. Fixed, ignorant attitudes have blocked proper social evolution because they deny the psyche openness and freedom to bloom. Montessori dedicated her efforts to children simply because she believed them to be neglected and abused from the moment of conception on.

She also felt that the natural joy of work had been lost to many adults. Much of work had become product-oriented, the criterion being who can do the least amount in the minimum time. Only some adults, such as artists, discoverers, explorers, and reformers maintain that irresistible impulse to work, which Montessori believed a true biological instinct. The child, she found, had the innate desire to work and did so effortlessly, when allowed to work under the proper conditions. In this vein the Montessori school

I came upon for my children was named The Child's Work Center affording a sharp contrast to the connotations of a play school.

Montessori saw work linked closely with the personality. Work is the mode in which the inner mind and spirit express themselves in the external environment. If this relationship doesn't exist, then the work is artificial and has no relation to the person's growth. Work also demands to be done in its own time to allow the personality to organize itself. Humans have to apply long mental efforts to mastering the complex voluntary muscles of their body in order to achieve perfection in detailed movement. A child learning to write is a prelude to the surgeon performing an operation.

The Montessori school, therefore, creates an environment where children may be seriously involved in activity, or work. Ideally Montessori considered her schools extensions of the home adapted to the children's, rather than adult's needs. They were also oases for the children from the many sensations bombarding them in the big world outside. Here the children could sort out their impressions, make exact distinctions, and develop their wills through the power of choice. Confidence is to be built up, rather than undermined.

Again and again Montessori said the requirement of a school was to maintain joy in life. She knew that many schools could teach subjects well but also leave the children without joy. She felt therefore that conditions had to be exact or else this spirituality would not occur in the children. Unlike administrators of other school systems, she saw no need for more extensive equipment, impressive buildings, innovative techniques. The basic requirements of a Children's House were simple rooms, access to a garden, children's-sized tables, chairs, rugs, and tools that related to the broad tasks of the world. When prepared by knowing Montessori directresses, these environments are beautiful in their ordered complexity and enriching aesthetic qualities.

Montessori's environmental concepts are related to her observations of the stages of human growth, the vital sensitive periods, cultural materials (meticulously selected and many designed by her), the role of the teacher/directress and other adults, and her understanding of the relationship among liberty, will and obedience. The Children's House for children aged two and one-half to five years, as well as the schools' advanced curriculum for children through twelve, reflect those insights.

Montessori divided the stages of mental and physical growth as follows. The first stage is from conception to three years and is called the absorbent mind in its *unconscious* mode. The second is from three to six and is called the absorbent mind in its *conscious* mode. The third stage is from six to twelve, the fourth is the adolescent from twelve to fifteen. And the fifth is maturity after adolescence. Each stage is characterized by the manifestation of different sensitive periods, behavior patterns and rhythms; each stage is to be met by suitable approaches. Environment is a crucial factor in the development of intelligence. Montessori believed that neither a tree nor a child could be forced to grow. The right environment could be provided only by observing how the child grew and what she needed.

In the first stage the psychic embryo passes from a tiny cell to a being that lifts her head, walks, talks, and learns to name objects. Montessori wrote:

> **In man the psyche must first construct the human faculties, which are not there (except potentially) at birth; and develop, too, those movements that serve these faculties. That is why the human embryo is born incomplete, physically, because the individual must wait, before beginning its movements, until the psyche has constructed itself, so that the body may develop as servant to the spirit.**

These are special sensitivities of this period. The infant's absorbent mind is intensely active on the unconscious level, absorbing sounds heard, shapes of objects, meaningful gestures or manners and innumerable other impressions. The child's family, an extension of the mother's womb, is meant to be loving, protective and nourishing so that the child can take in the new surroundings comfortably. The child does not think of herself as *I,* has no development of will and is totally dependent. Yet, this infant is not unintelligent and must be taken and shown about as much as possible. Her first major work is to absorb impressions of the environment.

Of the infant's transition from the unconscious to the conscious mode Montessori says:

> **If you watch a small child of two, he is always manipulating something. This means that — while he is manipulating with his hands — he is bringing**

**into consciousness what his subconscious mind had
already taken in before. It is through this experience
of objects in his environment, in the guise of playing, that he goes over again the impressions that he
has already taken in with his unconscious mind. It
is by means of this** *work* **— for it is as much work
as play — that he becomes conscious, and constructs
himself. He develops himself by means of his hands,
using them as the instruments of human intelligence.**

The more self-aware child from three to six can classify and
remember the impressions she takes in through her senses. As her
brain now directs her hand, her ego directs her choice of activity.
She enthusiastically learns from the family and the Children's House
habits of cleanliness, washing hands, dressing, care for belongings,
how to use eating utensils. The special sensitivities of this period
reveal themselves in what the child wants to do. If the child is cut
off from her interests, she will be more helpless and inadequate
later. At this age the child is universally sensitive to sharing things
with others and being responsible and participative. She wants to be
part of the group and wants the environment to be alive, responsive
to her. Love and respect for persons and things are now naturally
developed. The child's spontaneous curiosity and enthusiasm for the
world before six is there to be nurtured. She has developed discipline
and some capacity for abstract thought. She learns writing, reading,
fundamental concepts about numbers, and many other elements of
culture without fatigue through independent work.

The third epoch of growth is from six to twelve years. Before
six a child is interested in the facts about the world, now she wants
to know more about the whys, hows and consequences of the facts.
This is the period when sensorial data give way to the overall curriculum described earlier as Cosmic Education. Learning becomes the
study of the relationship among things, exploring the evolution of
plants, animals, humanity and the geological eras. Physically the
children are lankier; their second set of teeth is coming in. They
are strong, robust and calm. They are precise in their interest and
busy with their own affairs. They also form happy groups and are
anxious to explore life outside the classroom. It is a time for great
shoring up of cultural information, when rational and ethical faculties
are awakening. Through education of the cosmos the child learns the

unity of all things and sees her place in it. She sees that no isolation exists because all elements are dependent on others.

When a child reaches twelve, according to Montessori, she enters the difficult period of adolescence. Significant physical changes occur, physiologically generating doubts, hesitations, violent emotions, hostility to criticism, and the desire to be treated with respect. Montessori writes:

> **For example, a feeling of inferiority at this period may give rise to an *inferiority complex;* and there may arise a repugnance to social life which may endure for years. Such defects in social adjustment may have dangerous consequences for the individual, resulting in timidity, anxiety, depression. Bad results may follow for society too in the form of incapacity for work, laziness, dependence on others, a cynical outlook, and even criminality. Here, in the problem of social adjustment, lies the really vital problem of education for the adolescents, far more so than in the passing of examinations. (Erdkinder)**

In **Erdkinder (Children of the Earth),** Montessori describes the most suitable environment for children of this age. It is based on her idea that the adolescent needs to understand the society she is about to enter and at the same time be protected during this period of transformation. She proposed youth settlements set up in country districts where youth live communally and have modified economic independence. This country school is to offer fresh air, farm food, and good exercise. The young people are responsible for its maintenance and organization; they learn how to deal with financial obligations by raising animals, farming, and selling their products in nearby towns. In this way they learn the fundamentals of production and exchange in economic society. The community studies farming as it has evolved throughout the ages. Chemistry, law, physics, geology, geography, biology, cosmology, botany, zoology, astronomy and engineering are studied in tandem. The intellectual studies accompany practical experience in a miniaturized society. Montessori expressed the views of many modern educators and students when she wrote:

> **Young people in the secondary schools are compelled to study as a *duty* or a *necessity.* Their best individual energy is wasted. They are not working with interest**

**nor any definite aims that could be immediately
fulfilled and would give them satisfaction and a
renewed interest in the continuous effort . . .
Study becomes a heavy load that burdens the
young life instead of being felt as the privilege of
initiation to the knowledge that is the pride of
our civilization. The young people are formed into
a mold of narrowness, artificiality and egotism.**

One of Montessori's original ideas is to have a machine museum
where youth could take apart, reassemble, use and repair all types of
machines. The essential feature is for them to understand the use of
machines, to learn that the machines are not their masters nor instruments of ill purposes. Machines are to be familiar to them, used as
tools in the service of humanity. Her plan, which is akin to some
boarding schools in this country, offers an exciting solution to
adolescent depression problems. The young people are given real
responsibility and freedom in a secure, rich environment.

The post-adolescent youth is ready for the university or a vocation. In the university Montessori strongly opposed institutional or
faculty repression of students reacting to social injustice or to political
questions. She said that **such narrow minded authority would leave
young people with their minds so shackled and sacrificed to alien
pressures that they lose all power of individuation and can no longer
judge the problems of the age in which they live.**

Maturity is the time when all the seeds that were sown in childhood now flower. The young person is above seeking personal
possessions and positions of power. She wants a strong, rich and
purified world. She knows how to pursue her own course of action
and is aware of the potentialities and responsibilities of life. She
knows culture is never ended and that she has to find out how far
she is going to work in it for the sake of all humanity. Ideally, she
is beautiful in physical grace, living habits, and intellectual qualities.
She enjoys social life and always has the needs of others before her.
She is calm, cultured, active. Whereas the child-youth perfects the
self using the environment as means, now the mature adult works to
perfect the environment, using the self as means.

Thus Montessori divided the phases of growth. Each phase is
noticeably distinguished by sensitive periods, which are the inner
guides to growth that insure the survival and evolution of the species.

Springing from the unconscious, sensitive periods are experienced as strong urges toward areas of knowledge, movement, expression and social activity. They manifest themselves when the child is allowed to develop according to her own pace and rhythm. We are so accustomed to schools imposing schedules that sensitive periods are often ignored. When a child, for example, is inwardly ready to absorb information about how plants grow, she'll experience a flood of interest in the garden or taking care of the plants in the window. Amidst the confusion in her mind is the desire to make distinctions, after which comes creative work. Montessori believed that if the child is permitted to follow these mind-absorptions her personality is permeated with ennobling qualities. The child's urge toward union with something of this world is filled with loving concentration from within the self. The self is incarnated in the object. Some describe the experience as finding the Tao, the synchronistic match or psychological equivalent. It is spontaneous and lasts as long as it needs to. Learning, done in this way, is very easy, joyous and life-enhancing.

In **The Secret of Childhood** Montessori shows how the process of a caterpillar's metamorphosis into a butterfly depends on vital impulses affecting each stage of development, which are dropped as soon as they are not needed. For instance, the just-born caterpillar has an instinctual sensitivity to light which leads it to search for food where it receives the light and food essential to growth. When the caterpillar has grown enough, the sensitivity to light ends. So, the child has impulses which direct her acts in the world, leading her to the psychic conquests which are really awesome, although largely taken for granted by adults. Montessori wrote:

> **When one of these psychic passions is exhausted, another is enkindled. Childhood thus passes from conquest to conquest in a constant rhythm that constitutes its joy and happiness. It is within this fair fire of the soul, which burns without consuming, that the creative work of our spiritual world is brought to completion. On the other hand, when the sensitive period has disappeared, intellectual victories are reported through reasoning processes, voluntary efforts, and the toil of research. And from the torpor of indifference is born the weariness**

of labor. This then is the essential difference between the psychology of a child and that of an adult. A child has a special interior vitality which accounts for the miraculous manner in which he makes his natural conquests; But if during his sensitive stage a child is confronted with an obstacle to his toil, he suffers a disturbance or even warping of his being, a spiritual martyrdom that is still too little known, but whose scars are borne unconsciously by most adults. (Secret of Childhood)

Scars are awkward movements, indecision, lack of appreciation of art, music, games, lack of color sense, being poor at figures, illegible handwriting, shyness, dependency on others. To avoid these the adult must diligently watch for the child's signals, largely by listening to her express her desires, and provide the materials and environment to meet the child's inner hunger.

The *prepared environment* in Montessori schools is a highly complex and intricately worked out structure of materials. It serves as the beehive, anthill, mammal's placenta in providing for the developing young. (See the illustration of *prepared paths to culture.)*

Each material is related to other materials, not in a rigid lock-step method of use, of going from A to B, but as in the web of life, with an organic relationship among them. Each material isolates the lesson to be learned; it clarifies by removing confusing impediments.

Adults who train to work with the materials spend an intensive year in courses, filling by hand numerous notebooks on the characteristics of the materials, their possibilities, and the philosophy behind their use. Abbreviated courses really short-change the adult and the child because it takes time to understand the value of materials, educationally and spiritually. Montessori defined specific requirements for materials to meet the needs of children and designed herself most of those found in Montessori schools. As an educator she alone thoroughly worked out in concrete tangible objects and systems her philosophical ideas, all of which reflect her reliance on brain-hand coordination.

One successful factor concerning the materials in the schools is that there usually is only one of each so that the children will be obliged to share things. Also Montessori never intended that the

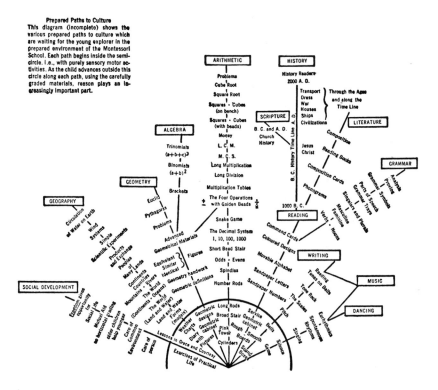

Prepared Paths to Culture
This diagram (incomplete) shows the various prepared paths to culture which are waiting for the young explorer in the prepared environment of the Montessori School. Each path begins inside the semi-circle. I.e., with purely sensory motor activities. As the child advances outside this circle along each path, using the carefully graded materials, reason plays an increasingly important part.

children scatter the materials about like loose dogs might. No, the materials are beautiful cultural tools, made out of fine polished wood, boxed in brightly color-coded cases and placed on open shelves. Everything is always kept clean and in good working order so that the child will not lose one moment of constructive mental energy. Montessori's objective is to generate energy in children, not to waste it. The materials are designed so that little explanation is required. They are usually presented to the children simply in the basic *3-period lesson:* 1. This is . . ., 2. Show me . . ., 3. What is this? Children then work with the material on their own, repeating it as often as they want to, allowing the eye-hand coordination to firmly implant itself on the intelligence. Sometimes the children are helped in their work by older ones; thus, a community of interests is encouraged. The child can work on a small rug placed on the floor, at a table, or even outdoors if the arrangement permits. The child is never to be interrupted while working, as that is when the spirit is flowing and all is well.

The specific materials and their aims are best described in **The Montessori Method** and **The Montessori Elementary Material.** According to Montessori's standards for the materials, they must have self-correcting factors, distinctions that make possible comparisons and judgements and permit independent repetitive work. Montessori felt that children should learn from the content of their own errors and build confidence in themselves by being able to find the correct way on their own. In other schools children make mistakes with indifference, because it is the teacher's business to correct them. The children are thus left dependent on the teacher for learning what is right, a situation that heightens indecisiveness through powerlessness. Montessori materials for the young are designed to meet the needs of children in practical life (bow-tying, lacing, sweeping, polishing, washing, etc.), social situations (asking for favors, serving table, respecting another's work, the desire to be beautiful, accepted and recognized); intellectual, cultural ways (language, sciences, writing, mathematics, etc.); and spiritual ways (religion, the arts). The Cosmic Education materials include such things as time-lines based on the beginning of the earth to the present, showing in pictures and words the evolution of plants, animals, human civilizations, geological eras. The history of subjects is given too, such as why and how the Hindus developed the system of decimals or how the alphabet grew, so that the child grasps the human need behind great accomplishments.

The materials' loftier purpose is, in unifying and strengthening the personality, to liberate the spirit. This is one of the primary reasons Montessori has unique distinction as an educator. This spirit, the psychic energy of children, was gold to her, and it was paramount to keep mining it. She compared the child also to a plant, saying a child takes in from the culture what is conducive to her growth, just as plants' roots select food from the soil.

> **It is often said that it is curiosity which stimulates these researches with the material. But it is not curiosity which urges the child, because when he has understood a thing, he no longer has intellectual**

curiosity with regard to it. So it is just when
curiosity is satisfied that there begins the real
expansive activity of the child. He does not now
act so that he may know, but that he may grow;
because he has need of action to reinforce and
expand his mind.

The child grows when there is deep inner involvement with the
material selected. Periods of involvement are thus sacred and
uninterruptible. They reveal themselves when the child is absorbed
in concentration on a piece of work to the extent of being unaware
of noises and activity surrounding her. Montessori likened the
process to meditation:

He who meditates clears his mind as far as
possible of every other image, and tries to
concentrate upon the subject of meditation
in such a manner that all the internal activities
will be polarised thereby: or, as the monks say,
all the powers of the mind.

The expected result of the meditation is *an
internal fruit of strength;* the soul is strengthened and unified, it becomes active; it can then
act upon the seed around which it has concentrated
and cause it to become fruitful.

Now the method chosen by our children in following
their natural development is *meditation,* for in no
other way would they be led to linger so long over
each individual task, and so to derive a gradual
internal maturation therefrom. The aim of the
children who persevere in their work with an object,
is certainly not to *learn;* they are drawn to it by
the needs of their inner life, which must be organized
and developed by its means. In this manner they
imitate and carry on their *growth.* This is the habit
by which they gradually coordinate and enrich their
intelligence. As they meditate, they enter upon that
path of progress which will continue without end.
(Spontaneous Activity In Education)

In this absorbed state Montessori felt children were most themselves, making fresh discoveries. (So she had seen in the child with
the little red string when she left medical school that day and came
upon the beggar woman and child.) Afterwards their energy is
refreshed and love for the world fills them. The spiritual benefits
are obvious.

Periods of intense absorption, Montessori discovered, follow
certain rhythmic patterns, depending upon the child and the task.
Work done according to personal rhythm makes one feel happy,
quite the opposite if one is forced to match the rhythm of another.
Rhythm is as intrinsic a fact of our lives as breathing; it reflects
the timetable of the inner organism, always present and functioning
in its calm way since birth. Montessori found variations in rhythm
patterns among children from rich and poor families, neglected or
over-stimulated. Most basically, however, a child working in a
disciplined way enters the school environment, keeps still for a
while, and then chooses some easy task. She works on this for a
short time, then finds something more difficult to do for a longer
time. At this point she rests, walks about the room, less calm,
giving the (false) impression of being tired, but then she undertakes
a more difficult work, and becomes deeply absorbed, reaching an
acme of activity. When she finishes, she is very serene and satisfied.
She then seeks someone out to talk to. Ordered activity, perse-
verance, and achievement are natural qualities.

Among American parents and educators a common criticism of
Montessori schools concerns art, since there is no special room for
it nor much organized pasting or crayoning. Actually Montessori
believed that the arts were the finest traces of civilization throughout
the ages. Her method for preparation in the arts was indirect,
dependent largely on the sensorial material that subtly distinguishes
relationships of color, prepares the muscles of the hand for writing
and drawing, sensitizes the ear through sound boxes and scales of
bell tones, and gives the body practice for controlling movement.
Art educators agree that proper aesthetic education consists of
education of the senses, upon which ultimately the intelligence and
judgement of the individual are based. Evaluated according to this
definition, the Montessori approach is most thorough. Furthermore,
art is the primary way of integration of perception and feeling, a
basic principle underlying Montessori's method.

A feature of the materials is that they demonstrate abstract concepts in concrete form. Thus, children, touching with their hands, and seeing with their eyes, truly get to understand the world. Children are grounded in reality. They do not escape into false illusory worlds, but rather they build their imaginations on solid principles. Montessori sought always to enflame the child's imagination with the magnificent realities of the world, to which all study contributed. Reality is the ground, take-off point, for the imagination to fly. Real creativity to her was the associative ability to make new syntheses among the elements. She opposed taking advantage of children's credulity and sincerity by dwelling on false stories. When children seek escape in vague fantasies, she thought that they are having trouble communicating with the world; they look disrupted and dislocated.

Good Montessori teachers cultivate in children the artistic impulse at all times by showing them examples of the finest art of all periods and peoples. A teacher, for example, might show the evolution of culture through the beautiful form and use of the vase and then bring clays for the children to make useful and ornamental things for themselves. Children are introduced to languages, the rhythm of syllables and rhyming words in poetry and prose. The children write and draw, guided by their own spirit. Montessori believed that the best instructor of the arts was really the inner self, which as it developed and experienced life, sought to be born externally. Thus, her emphasis was to refine the child's observation of nature so that the child would have a rich store of perceptions to work from. She felt that the more accurate and perfect the child's observations were, the more vigorous would be the form created. Because life is a better preparer of art than other teachers, the child's hand, eye, ear, soul should be made ready for the call of inner vision. She felt art developed this way would lead to much truer products of the soul than when the spirit was submitted to technical schools.

Of course, part of the child's cultural environment is the adult — as parent, teacher, relative, acquaintance. In Montessori schools the **teacher** is referred to as the *Directress,* because the adult is to be an observant, guiding person rather than one who forces the education-curriculum on children. In the Montessori way, the Directress is the entity who has the great responsibility of providing the right environment for the children and sensitively filling their spiritual and intellectual needs. She must create the atmosphere wherein a child can center herself. She must recognize the individual personalities of the children and assist their development. She has the air of being in service of the great future human being, and she acts unperverted by prejudice or political creed. She removes fear from the atmosphere, so that minds can study in freedom and open up toward what they love. She has faith that the child will reveal her spirit when the child finds work that attracts her.

Respecting the child's personality means allowing it to develop with as little assistance as possible, for to assist the child when she is trying to do it herself, even when the act seems clumsy and difficult, does the child an injury. Thus the helplessness and dependency of the child are prolonged. The Directress is the vital link between the children and the materials. Because a class consists ideally of around 40 children the Directress won't be tempted to interfere too much. She moves among the children rather than being fixed at a desk with their eyes upon her all day. All day her attention is focused on helping the children expand themselves through work and removing obstacles in their path. She reaches the deeper levels of the child, cutting through the superficialities of clumsy movements, vague ideas, resistances, in order to lead her into experiences. She stirs up the higher energies which are sleeping behind the surface mask, the energies which guide the children to wisdom and peace. She knows the differences between children's impulses and true spontaneity emanating from a tranquil spirit.

She corrects willful disordered movements by introducing movements which are interesting and lead to harmony. Wandering attention she focuses in physical reality. The tendency to imitate others she counters by developing the child's power of choice, decision, will. The Directress does not hesitate to stop disorderly behavior but she does it not by shaming or clamping down but by awakening the children to good, constructive behavior. She only gives lessons with the consent of the child. If the child is working on something, she would not say *that's good,* as that would express her control and make the child defensive.

According to Montessori, parents too should see themselves as guardians and protectors of children, rather than their makers. They should act as collaborators in the child's building process. This role does not diminish their importance, for a great deal of sensitivity is required to provide for the child's needs. Adults can show the child the active world of nature and can build up the child's language and culture through stories. Adults should stand behind the child. The child needs firm guidance to act responsibly, not of the authoritarian variety but intuitive, to help the child channel herself.

The mote in the eye of adults, preventing many from assuming this role, is that they regard as natural in children traits that Montessori considered deviations, such as weeping, shouting, tantrums, timidity, possessiveness, fibs, selfishness and destruction. To Montessori these are defenses of the child against the adult's aggressions on her being. The adult tries to eliminate these qualities by stern assaults, creating more defenses, a vicious circle. Any parent who has in the grip of emotion (often generated from an outside source) shouted at a child and forced her to do what the parent wanted for no reason other than selfish convenience must appreciate what is happening psychologically in the periods of silence or screaming that follow.

Whereas adults generally find it difficult to allow children to grow without controlling their *bad* behavior, Montessori believed that the child's whims, struggles, tantrums, even illness mean that a nobler trait is trying to break through. She proved again and again that behavioral problems disappear when the psychic laws innate in children are mandated. She did not mean to let loose wanton, chaotic expression of the instincts. She said that the individual must acknowledge and recognize anger, greed, and envy and harness them by integration with more acceptable, exalted impulses of life. Far better for human beings to develop according to the potentials given in relation to their time-space. Only the individual can find a workable way to unite her life with the demands of the culture.

When the child's nature is given freedom to unfold in an environment which helps her understand the culture and eventually play her part in the regenerative universe, when the child can spontaneously explore, seed, repair, read, etc., Montessori found that the child's personality is valorized. The child behaves in ways that are normal and sublime.

What is normal to Montessorians? The child is comfortably independent and associates with others easily. She loves to finish a

task rather than be idle. She responds eagerly to the process of
doing things repetitively and orderly, as well as making her own
choices. She does not seek approval nor require punishment. She
likes silence and becomes self-disciplined. She possesses inspiring
dignity, with an inner glow of light and calm.

Montessori is unique among educators in her emphasis on
developing the will. The will is closely related to the child's self-
discipline and developed in Montessori schools through the power
of choice and decision. Montessori adamantly deplored the ignorance behind the imposition of discipline from the outside. In
conventional schools children are made to sit still without talking
while subjects are force-fed. Some sports and defense training (i.e.,
army) reduce the human to a blob of protoplasm who must
perform certain motions but no others. Qualities such as passivity,
acquiescence, repression are cultivated. The person is left with no
will, a confused mind, and susceptible to being blown about by
life's circumstances or dominating figures. Such a person is a total
victim of the environment and a potential menace to society and
the earth. Montessori saw the essential need for the will to be
developed so that moral rightness was possible.

Thus, in her schools Montessori promoted an atmosphere that
fostered strengthening of self-discipline. First, teachers were
enjoined not to help a child unless she needed it, so that nature
could pursue its course in making the child self-sufficient.
Montessori gave the child freedom to move around the room, to
work on the floor, etc. so that her limbs could move and stretch.
She gave the same freedom to the child's psyche. Once a child is
shown how to use materials, she must choose among them, so
that her internal growth occurs at her own timeclock. Montessori
said, **The child who cannot obey an inner guide is not a free
being set on the long and narrow path to perfection, but still a
slave to sensations which leave her at the mercy of her environment.** Working with the materials she is free to associate, synthesize,
and reproduce results. In working the child cannot interfere with
the rights and desires of others. This freedom within limits produces
a considerate calm and happiness within the children, as well as a
feeling of mastery and accomplishment.

Children, given this character growth, can obey adults easily in
situations that call for it. Montessori observed three stages of

obedience in the child. The first stage is when the child is an infant and cannot obey because she has no will. The second stage is when she is two or three and may or may not obey a command, according to her impulse and not the will of the adult. When the child is six, she is able to carry out orders commensurate with her ability to do so. Thus, it happens that an order obeyed once may not be obeyed the second time, because the task is too difficult to be done twice in a row. She has to have acquired the skills, for example, to dress herself or set the table. Action or movement is important to the development of the will, because the child in directing a movement exercises her will to carry it out. Work involving muscular coordination increases the ability to control the self. Montessori analyzed the movements required in using materials, so that the child could be helped in choosing clear movements. Sometimes movements have to be restricted such as those of anger or of impulsively snatching something from someone, but the children's generous inclinations to be sociable, caring, and helpful are encouraged. The third stage is when the child is capable of turning to an older adult whom the child feels is superior because she wants to obey the adult. She is impatient and enthusiastic about obeying, having developed her will sufficiently to do so. And Montessori warns a good adult to be scrupulous in not taking advantage of this form of obedience. This obedience is characterized by the child's choosing to sublimate her will for that which she feels is better. Such grace cannot be achieved by command.

Maria Montessori's educational method is in essence her practical, workable solution to the failures found in society. Montessori was supremely concerned about the social institutions created by and for human beings. She addressed the United Nations, visited the leaders of countries all over the globe, and wrote volumes on her vision of society. Thus, all of her work must be seen in the context of her overall social philosophy.

First of all, Montessori considered adults presently the victims of their environment and this victimization the root of their problems. The child by contrast is a natural being, undamaged by false assumptions and degrading circumstances, with the potential psychic energy to guide humanity in its future successful adaptation to the earth. Adults comprising society, however, act as a kind of collective unconscious to ignore and suppress the child. Montessori termed hypocritical adults' talk of love and sacrifice for their children. Their rationalizations incited future parents to absorb negative attitudes toward children and sanction their actions. Thus, generation after generation mental barriers are erected against the child. Not only are repressive attitudes to children passed on, but also prejudices about work and other peoples, including families and nations. Society in institutionalizing these prejudices effectively buries the actual potential of human beings.

Child-raising today is often taken for granted or regarded as a chore. Fortunately, rather than project their conflict on children, many adults today question whether they should even have children, and are effectively able to bypass the experience. In countries where birth control methods are not used widely, bearing children is still the biological destiny of life, a view that is still firmly implanted in the minds of women even in America where birth control is easily available. The level of child abuse everywhere is still frighteningly high. Not only are children tortured physically, but also psychologically by all levels of society. Children are verbally insulted, rejected, and manipulated. Many parents assume their responsibility ends with providing food and clothes. They strive to get away from their children as much as possible. In divorce cases parents exchange them for a lump of money. Yet having shown themselves to be passive and insensitive, parents cannot understand why their children want to run away from home.

Montessori felt that adults' behavior toward children reflects their psychological blindness. Adults simply cannot *see* the nature of the child because of hidden fears, often unacknowledged by their conscious minds. Until adults unlock those fears, conflicts with children will continue. Montessori strongly advocated that parents-to-be receive instruction about the child's nature before they conceive children, so that they can be prepared to receive children properly. Addressing the Italian government she said,

> **The state, so rigorous in demanding official documents and meticulous preparations and which so loves to regulate everything that bears the smallest trace of social responsibility, does not trouble to ascertain the capacity of future fathers to give adequate protection to their children or to guard their development.**

**It has provided no place of instruction or preparation
for parents. As far as the state is concerned, it is
enough for anyone wishing to found a family to go
through the marriage ceremony. In view of all this
we may well declare that society from earliest times
has washed its hands of those little workers to whom
nature has entrusted the task of building up humanity.**

The roles of mothers and fathers must be more supportive. The
answer is not in confining the child to the home with the mother.
This arrangement began not so much out of consideration for the
child, but from a patriarchal attitude to keep women out of the
work force. The child needs companionship from mothers, fathers,
relatives, and people in all walks of life. Too frequently fathers
abandon their children to pursue a heavy schedule of business and
recreation. Because both men and women need meaningful work in
their lives, which the child can observe, society can make it easier
for families by permitting flexible working hours and accommodations.
Society should have a stake in its future citizenry. Child-raising is
much too important to be consigned to the parents' few hours at
the end of an exhausting work day. It is a responsibility to be
conducted with honor and enthusiasm. Parents and all adults should
be able to spend time talking and planning activities with children.
Not only should this be done to create a better climate for
children's growth, but also so that the adult may learn from the
child, for as Montessori said:

**We began by protecting the child and now we
realize that it is we who need protecting. We began
with methods of education and culture for the child,
and we end by acknowledging that he is our teacher.
Not a teacher who gives us culture, but one who can
reveal to us, as no other, our own nature and its
possibilities . . . The child is an authority: and the
adult must make himself in accord with this authority
if he wishes to better his conditions . . . By changing
the centre from the adult — and adult values — to
the child, and his values we should change the whole
path of civilization.**

But social institutions from the beginning of a child's existence
reveal woefully inadequate views toward the child. Consider the

hospital where the infant must by law be born. When the mother-to-be arrives, she carries the precious embryo in her. For nine months her health has been of the utmost concern, so that the complex needs of this psychic organism can be nourished in growth from conception. The embryo has hopefully prospered in the natural liquids of the womb. Now that it is to be transferred to a larger environment, what is provided by advanced health care in our hospitals? The pregnant mother is often subjected to the convenience of the doctor. When she arrives at the hospital, she is taken over by assistants doing their duty routinely with no trace of ceremony. Women are often drugged to either speed up or retard their labor pains, according to the doctor's convenience. Women have been given drugs, such as scopolamine, which causes lasting damage. In birth the mother is laid out prone with arms strapped and legs raised and locked in stirrups. She is imprisoned and often knocked unconscious. This is a far cry from nature's planned birth position. Nature's way is an upright crouch, but that is not comfortable for the doctors. Nature does not plan to have babies pried out with forceps nor the afterbirth forced out right away. The natural environment has been greatly modified by man.

And what are the effects on the baby, just emerged from the tender, warm womb? She is rudely spanked, dunked roughly in water, and shocked by light and cold. If a boy he may be circumcized, a brutal operation that may cause hidden psychic damage. Montessori urged that infants be left naked, warmed and protected by their mothers' bodies, as are animal babies. Clothes are not as efficient as the body warmth, because they simply retain the heat from the area of the body covered, leaving exposed to the elements the face, hands, etc. Montessori felt the newborn should be handled as a sacred object. The baby should be moved gently because sudden movements create fears of falling, and the baby should be left with the mother rather than taken away. Sometimes it is hard to convince the hospital staff that a mother nurse her baby, obliging the mother to fight for her natural right. The immaculate conveniences of the hospital have overlooked the basic requirements of the human infant, by not providing an environment rich with nourishment, warmth and love, as close as possible to womb conditions, so that the baby can comfortably adapt to its new life in the world.

The next institution the growing child confronts is the day care center or school. Presently day care centers are ineptly planned so that they are just repositories for as many children as possible, with televisions set up in warehouse-size rooms, offering no chance for a child to have solitude or privacy. Schools are now mandatory for all children and sometimes seem like prisons. Parents transfer their problems with their children to the teachers and principals; they are happy to be free of the burden of children. The wealthy choose a private school too often because it is the thing to do, where the *right people* are, rather than for its educational benefits. In public and private schools children too often lose their sense of identity and place in the world, growing progressively more insecure in a system that will not bend to help. For many children their day is spent resisting and defending themselves against adults. The task of re-orienting them to their natural curiosity and joy in life is enormous, requiring degrees of love and understanding that many of us are not capable of. Even when a school is run along Montessori's principles, the cure of the deviations is difficult and time-consuming.

To work for the future of humanity to Montessori meant devoting oneself to children. She thought that great strides had been made in liberating children from the superstitions surrounding their physical growth. Adults no longer bound children's limbs so they would grow straight; it was accepted that nature took care of this best in unhindered growth. Noses were not pinched, clothing loosened, all permitted more freedom for the body to grow of itself. But about psychic needs Montessori felt that the general awareness of people was still in the Dark Ages. The psyche was not trusted to have freedom. Montessori's work in anthropology, medicine, science and education gave her the power to apprehend the physical and psychic unity of the human organism. She had highly refined techniques which were really more valuable than the conclusions she made, for conclusions are always in flux, but the ability to be open and observant is a constant necessity.

To increase support and concern for the child Montessori endeavored to establish a worldwide ministry of the child. She and her followers termed it the Social Party of the Child. The world wars had taught Montessori the devastation of nationalism, the superficialities in the politics of people claiming to be

Bolshevist, Fascist or Democrat. By living in many countries
Montessori saw how economic competition and the struggle for
superiority left people in greatly contrasting states of poverty or
gross materialism. Morality seemed at a cynical low point in that
people followed leaders who brought their nations to disaster, and
people had such uncontrolled wills that they could not cooperate
with their government and sought only revolt. Since society however is dependent on cooperation from its people, the wills of the
people must be awakened and exercised, so that obedience can be
consciously given. Montessori wrote:

> . . . **every good thing, all progress, all discoveries**
> **can increase the evil afflicting the world, as we**
> **have seen in the case of machines and atomic**
> **energy. Every discovery that might mean elevation**
> **and progress can be used for destruction, for war,**
> **for self-enrichment . . . We have therefore nothing**
> **to hope from the external world till the normaliza-**
> **tion of man is recognized as the basic achievement**
> **of social life.**

As humans it is futile to ignore each other and the earth. No
one nation can survive without the produce and labor of other
nations. The world, Montessori said, is like one body with limbs
performing different functions; commerce and trade and monetary
exchanges are like the blood coursing through its veins. Some signs
of emerging world unity, she felt, were apparent in the formation
of the United Nations, but far greater willful recognition of the
interdependence of the world's parts is essential for the earth's
continuity. Montessori's hope lay always in the children.

> . . . **it follows that, if we wish to alter the habits**
> **and customs of a country, or if we wish to accen-**
> **tuate more vigorously the characteristics of a people,**
> **we must take as our instrument the child, for very**
> **little can be done in this direction by acting upon**
> **adults. To change a generation or nation, to influence**
> **it towards either good or evil, to re-awaken religion or**
> **add culture, we must look to the child, who is**
> **omnipotent.**

Montessori saw that the education of children was the basis for
the reconstruction of society and armament for peace. She is as

important to the cause of peace as Gandhi; indeed they were
exactly the same age and admirers of each other. In her work with
children she felt international understanding of peoples already
existed. In children hate did not take root; feelings of hostility are
accepted and put aside in favor of a larger goal. She saw in children
a natural tendency to appreciate the ecology of life, to want to
preserve rather than destroy. Children have to be taught prejudice,
for it is far more instinctual with them to feel part of the whole
human family.

Because humans grow up to be victimized by society, Montessori
felt the need for their reconstruction is paramount. Many adults
despise the routine of their work. War threatens their lives. Money is
not safe; it may be here today and gone tomorrow. Basic energy
resources can be depleted. People resort to cheating and robbing in
order to eat. Jobs are highly uncertain. People in a democracy are
no more free than others to take initiative against the established
powers. There is world illiteracy and starvation. People are depressed,
insecure, frightened and suspicious. Montessori's method of education
helps people preserve their psychic balance and build up security in
the present circumstances of the world. It demands the cooperation
among many people, so that it can raise humanity above its present
level.

To Montessori a Cosmic Education would produce the two
essentials for a reconstructed peaceful society: a new type of person
and a world environment accessible and responsible to all. The new
person burns with spiritual purpose. She is a citizen of the world
and is concerned with preserving natural resources, the making of
useful products, and the formation of the young. She has been
normalized through work which means cured of emotional deviations
through being in touch with her own relationship to the environment. She leads a simple life with a strong love and understanding
for living beings. She does not define love by her willingness to
die on the battlefield fighting for others but by her *preservation* of
life and the land. Beyond political ideology, she is devoted to the
future of humanity. She serves the cosmos.

The adult of the world, Montessori thought, would likely form
communities in which man, woman and child are involved in the
necessary tasks. Relatives would be close to the children; neither
school nor work places would be separate from the home. Agrarian

workers would work more in conjunction with factory workers and business executives would not be a separate group enjoying special privileges. The community itself would be like a body in miniature. Materials and tools would be shared, the instinct to possess becoming instead a desire to know, to love, and to serve the object. People would use each other's energy, seeing each other as extended parts of themselves. Montessori's ideas can be seen in William Irwin Thompson's definition of the emerging community:

> **And so if in the sixties we saw the formation of the nuclear individual as institution, I would expect to see in the seventies the formation of the community as individual. This would not be the bee in the beehive of Mao's China, but a culture in which the depth of a person's individuation describes the very nature of his bond with the group. As electrons become a single gas in the super-conducting state, so men in the divinely superconducting state would become a single cosmic consciousness.**

In 1964 Montessori said, **The child who is developing harmoniously with the adult, who is thus elevated by his closeness to him, makes a gripping vision.** Maria Montessori envisioned a society in which all of us are children of the cosmos. Adults who have grasped this now quietly and thoroughly meet the challenges of our day as parents, teachers, or just plain friends of children, from remotest Africa to urbanized America. They know that the same energy that generates the world activates the human psyche. In constructing themselves and the future of the world, they absorb the world culture's information and tools as well as possess a strong center within themselves from which they pursue their work. For such people the task of life is not just a practical necessity; it is also a step in the evolution of the cosmos, and they are pilgrims. Montessori was joyfully aware of this in her response to a query about her nationality: **I live in Heaven, my country is a star which turns around the sun and is called the Earth.**

Frances Steloff

The Power Within

The Gotham Book Mart is a famous literary bookshop in New York. It is presently located at 41 West 47th Street, in the heart of the jewelers' district. This bookshop is the only gem on the street that fascinates me. It was founded in 1920 by Frances Steloff, who at 88 years of age has become an institution. My visits to the Gotham Book Mart and long conversations with Frances Steloff are part of a quest to piece together the puzzle of this woman and her life-time dedication to books. By examining the key persons, the decisions made at crossroads, the images that inspired her, I hope to present the fabric of her life. But above all I am interested in the power within Frances Steloff that shaped the fabric, as a needle guides the thread bit by bit producing the design, which is not fully discernible until a life or design is really finished. Because the Gotham Book Mart has epitomized my love for literature, as I read, write and publish, and because she, as a woman, started her business and brought it to its present level of distinction, my interest acquires many dimensions.

Just walking to the Gotham Book Mart, I become more excited the closer I get. My eyes spot first the antique cast-iron sign hung out in front with her motto *Wise Men Fish Here* below a plate of three men catching a big fish. I reach the front window that spans almost the width of the building. Every week the display is different. Today the theme focuses on the witty, surreal works of Marcel Duchamp, Lewis Carroll and Edward Gorey. I am reminded that Frances Steloff told me how Marcel Duchamp and André Breton arranged a now famous display for Breton's book **Arcane 17.** A representative from the vice squad considered a portion objectionable, so over the objectionable spot Steloff placed his card reading *CENSORED,* which created more of a sensation than ever.

Steloff has always considered the window displays valuable. One story about them reflects how her mind was opened by the artists and writers who came into her domain. Peggy Guggenheim and Max Ernst came in, seeking to have a display of Peggy Guggenheim's new book, **Art of This Century,** in the Gotham Book Mart window. Steloff was not interested in the surrealist art but agreed to think about it. She opened the book to an image of Pevsner's *Surface Developing a Tangency with a Left Curve,* which seemed more marvellous in detail and execution the more she looked at it. She was so amazed, she even wanted to buy it. The experience made her realize how people are cheated because of their prejudices or failure to be receptive to the artist or poet.

Another time she went to great lengths to arrange a special window exhibit on women writers, for which she had a sawhorse made which read in bold letters — **Women at Work.**

Part of every window display includes a row of 20 to 30 of the latest literary magazines, which Steloff has indefatigably supported. She believes that writers, literary connoisseurs, and editors flock to the Gotham Book Mart because of these magazines. Writers come to see their own work and editors find exciting writers whose work lends itself to book form. Because editors benefit so much from the literary magazines, Steloff is convinced that book publishers should underwrite them financially. The Gotham Book Mart's collection of magazines is especially precious because many drop out of existence every year because of financial or other hardships.

I enter the building, which houses the Gotham Book Mart. The building also contains Frances Steloff's two-room apartment on the third floor, and between the shop and the apartment is the Gotham Gallery, which is the scene for parties, lectures, and literary organization meetings. Steloff lives with her work. Indeed, she would not have to go out at all, for her whole life goes on in that space. Such unity is important to her; it is more than a convenience.

The Gotham inside is a total environment. Even the dust is atmospheric. Thousands of books fill wooden bookcases and the floor creaks as I walk among them. The aura is thick with the art of writing as thoughtful vocation, more so than money-making career or technical scholarly endeavor. Here I am among those whose books are from the passionate heart. In this bookship there are no general cookbooks (except for specialized ones, such as vegetarian), no how-to, no games, no jewelry, no stationery. Neither the publishers' blockbusting best-sellers, nor children's books are heavily promoted here, only the books that publishers generally consider the most unprofitable. And yet this bookshop is in its 55th year of doing steady business around the world with those who order in- and out-of-print books by the important modern authors. The Gotham Book Mart's horde of first editions, manuscripts, letters, literary magazines, mostly stored in crowded stockrooms and in the basement, has been called by many *the most significant literary archive of the twentieth century.* Recently the Gotham Book Mart sold at least 200,000 items for $485,000 to New Mexico State University.

I check out a bulletin board displaying notices of poetry readings, contests, and new publications. Then the top of the front shelf, on which are the latest issues of *The American Poetry Review, Fiction, New York Review of Books,* and books fresh from publishers' cartons. The place bustles with the activity of customers. The kindly woman at the cash register smiles at me. A harried salesboy rushes by, muttering titles. In the back room, housing the literary magazines and scores of books alphabetized by author's names, a man dictates a letter.

I walk past shelves in the front room beneath photographs of D.H. Lawrence, Gertrude Stein, and Kay Boyle. Once upon a time some young authors protested being shelved next to those considered old-fashioned, but now a comfortable mix has been established. There also used to be a section called the *Wailing Wall* that consisted of books ordered by the Gotham Book Mart with unwarranted enthusiasm. People have browsed among the labyrinth of books for years, pleasantly surprised to surface with titles that they never knew they wanted. I reluctantly pass onward, but with a minute's pause at the popular theatre and film books, to my favorite section, a small room with shelves of books on philosophy, psychology, religion, mysticism, and the occult. Tacked on a wall is a sign no visitor can miss. It says, **Shoplifters, remember your karma.** There is also a desk, piled nearly two feet high with papers, including unopened mail. Frances Steloff herself is there, peering closely at her social calendar.

This 88-year-old woman has thick white hair tied back with a blue scarf. She wears a purple and white silk dress which fits loosely around her body. An apron is tied around her waist. She spies me.

Hello-o-o, she says, welcoming me warmly. She grins expectantly, while I lean over to kiss her warm cheek and momentarily enfold her narrow shoulders. At 5' 6" I stand a head above her. **Well, my dear, how nice!,** she says and perches on the piano stool that serves as her chair. For awhile she is silent, contemplating me with lively blue-green eyes. She assesses my mood and the meaning of my presence. For her, silences are when a person's inner essence speaks loud and clear, louder than if the person were to talk about him/ herself. I wait too to see if she must take flight into other duties, or if she will stay with me. Some people misinterpret this action by thinking her hearing is weak. Instead she seems guided by her instincts.

I want to show you a letter from Skidmore College. They are giving me an honorary Doctorate of Humane Letters. Can you imagine! She searches through the piles of papers on the desk. As she hopelessly looks in all the drawers, I note the remarkable softness and smoothness of her skin. She is extraordinarily healthy. Only once in years have I seen her ill. She had a cold and her cure was to go on a two-day fast. She thinks that her diet kept her body from getting old, although she feels she has overworked her eyes and ears. Wisps of white hair fall out of place, hinting at the constancy of her hard work. After a while she stands stalwartly in custom-fitted shoes, holding not the letter but a book on psychic healing.

Frances Steloff holds a book in her strong arms the way an ancient Mother/Goddess would hold the white bone from which humans are created. A book to Steloff is the highest embodiment of the human heart and soul. It represents culture and civilization. To books and the people who worked on them Steloff dedicated her life as totally and devotedly as a nun in a cloister. Her bookshop was her spiritual proving ground with rituals requiring inner discipline. Years of practical necessity, care and inner passion forged her spirit.

Suddenly Steloff exclaims, **Oh, there's Bucky!** And in an instant she has dashed over to embrace Buckminster Fuller, a friend of the Gotham Book Mart for decades. Both figures are about the same height. Both have the same gentleness and for a moment are at a loss for words, although their eyes glisten. For each of them New York has surely been warmed up by the other's presence. They talk for half an hour, delighting in each other's news, while I seize the time to browse through some bookshelves.

Frances Steloff has surmounted great obstacles in carving out a career in a traditionally man's world. She overcame having no money, schooling that ended at the seventh grade, and persistent discouragement. She is an inspiration to those who fear they have no skills. Though her story is a courageous one, she herself attributes her success to a **string of miracles.** Again and again she has told me about an **invisible plan** at work in her life.

In coming to learn about Steloff's relationship to work, I find that others have seen her as a model of the successful businesswoman. One woman wrote her, **I am always looking for real life women through whom my daughter can see how much she and life have to give each other. So I hope I can bring her to meet you.** Steloff developed an iron will in tenaciously persevering toward her goals. Her terms consisted in not following popular commercial trends such as *hard-sell* advertising, or the supermarket type of store, or franchising. Yet, whereas presidents of publishing conglomerates find her enterprise financially negligible, these same men — leading booksellers, editors, and heads of writers' organizations — speak of her with respect and admiration.

Bucky Fuller is spotted by some customers who ask for his autograph. Steloff returns to me and says, **Let's talk upstairs.** She picks up her thermos of herb tea and leads the way up the stairs.

As always she pauses on the second-floor landing of the Gallery and says that I really must see the current exhibit — this time photographic portraits of contemporary poets on a wall. At the landing is a poster-sized blow-up of the *Life Magazine* photograph of the Gotham Book Mart's reception for Dame Edith and Sir Osbert Sitwell, which includes W.H. Auden, Marianne Moore, Randall Jarrell, Stephen Spender, Tennessee Williams, and Gore Vidal. The photograph best symbolizes the parties given by the Gotham Book Mart for three generations of famous authors, who have considered the Gotham Book Mart the most important place for their books to be sold, to have a publication party, and to meet kindred spirits.

I first glimpsed Frances Steloff at a lecture given in the Gallery. Charles Poncé, an author of several books on the **I Ching,** alchemy, and mysticism, was to speak on *Symbolism and Death,* New York's *Village Voice* announced. My literary antennae picked it up. This was ten years after I had first heard of Frances Steloff in college. She and Sylvia Beach of Paris were often compared, both having been born in the same year and on different continents starting famous *literary* bookshops. The aura of bohemian and beaux-arts literary life was always heavy stuff for me and now that I had established a small press myself, I was guided there straightaway.

When I arrived, I relaxed in the comfortable, intimate, bookish atmosphere. Poncé, wearing a handsome maroon velvet jacket, spoke softly on the transformation of the self to about twenty people. On the walls were E. E. Cummings' watercolors of beach scenes. Immediately I surmised (correctly) that Frances Steloff was the woman sitting in the front row with her hand cupped to her ear to hear better and holding a white cat in her lap. For a while the cat sat in my lap and when I returned him to his owner, I didn't at all mind the hairs clinging to my coat.

Little did I expect to really get to know this famous old lady. The very next day I attended a workshop given at a hotel by Dr. Ira Progoff on the *Intensive Journal,* a psychological notebook. Coincidentally two women poets were there who were friends of Frances Steloff, as I discovered in the morning break. Late in the afternoon I was writing in a section of the Journal called *Dialogue with Wisdom Figures.* Although I really knew nothing about her, I chose to have an imaginary talk with Frances Steloff, as one to whom I could discuss my wishes and problems freely. Undoubtedly

I had chosen her because she was on my mind from the day before and represented the literary scene. All of a sudden I looked up and there she was sitting near me writing in a Journal herself! I was so stunned that we had the experience of Progoff's Journal in common that I excitedly went over to tell her how I had chosen to dialogue with her and that then she appeared. She was delighted and remarked about the **beginning** of things. Truly, it not only was the beginning of Spring, but also of our relationship.

Soon after that my partner in the Press and I approached Steloff about participating in a weekend symposium we planned with Anais Nin and other authors, critics, magazine editors and publishers in her life. When we arrived at the Gotham Book Mart to take Frances Steloff to dinner, she said **I never say no to anything.** Characteristically she added, **But why me? I am not important.** She threw a blue Quaker-style cloak around her shoulders and hastily went out the door, leaving us to keep up if we could. She amazed us by threading her way among moving cars going in both directions before we even started to cross the street. Throughout the dinner she mostly listened to us. Her only comment was that she would hate to miss a memorial meeting for Madame Blavatsky scheduled near the same date. I had the feeling we were being tested.

At the weekend celebration with Anais Nin, my partner, who shared a room with Steloff, marvelled at Steloff's serenity, saying that when Frances went to bed, she would cover her face with a sheet and fall asleep instantly. Also, each evening at sunset Frances Steloff sat on a bench, huddled in a coat, and meditated upon the cosmic drama. When she gave her talk to the crowd, who had come from all over the country, she quipped at the start, **Anais Nin liberated me at 85,** referring to the fact that although she had known Nin for 30 years, she just read her **Diaries** and found them helpful. Then she sat in a chair to reminisce, wearing a yellow dress and lavender sandals. In her hand she held three dandelions to center on. Her stories about the Gotham, humbly told and filled with details, inspired everyone.

At the end of the weekend she said she realized why we asked her to participate. All the publishers and literary magazine editors and authors had said the first thing they did with their books was take them to the Gotham Book Mart. Seeing their books at the

Gotham was more important to them than any other place. Their appreciation finally made a tangible impression.

As we ascend the steps to the third floor, I feel as though we are leaving behind Steloff's world of action and about to cross the threshold of her private life. Another sign, this one over the panelled door to her apartment, boldly states: **If you love animals, don't eat them!** One of Steloff's major activities at present is organizing benefits for saving animals from slaughter and extinction. She criticizes my leather briefcase and checks to see that my coat is made of wool. Her greatest ambition is to liberate animals for their sake and ours. For, as she maintains, behind animal, vegetable, and human forms we are all part of One Consciousness. **When we hurt any one of us, it doesn't matter when or where, the same shall be returned to us. And when we think about this, we will realize our true Oneness.**

Steloff unlocks the door to her apartment, saying, **The cats live here, you know. I'm only a guest.** No sooner do I step inside then I nearly stumble over one of the half dozen dishes of food placed around for the two white cats. Although Steloff is a strict vegetarian, she does not force her philosophy onto her cats. Their food comes from the restaurants Steloff frequents, where the waitresses give her bags to take home. The cats, twins, are both called *Putsy.*

The apartment, which I have visited before, remains a wonder to me. Its two rooms are heaped with papers, books, photographs, and small objects arranged on shelves and tables. Boxes of memorabilia lay open on the floor. A tiny television screen peeks out from under a sheaf of papers and books. The floor is bare, except for a thin dark rug in a corner. One Putsy lies on a pile of letters on the desk, a living paperweight. Prints of the famous elegant houses of Saratoga Springs hang on the wall, amidst personally inscribed photographs of Henry Miller, Martha Graham, and Katherine Anne Porter. A pair of French windows, banked by a few plants and a sculptured bust of a woman, opens onto a small terrace overlooking the street. On hot summer nights Steloff still sleeps on the terrace. In the bedroom are more bookshelves, including a vast collection of old texts from India. Dusty boxes and more stacks of books crowd Steloff's cot, which is covered with a faded maroon coverlet and dark cushions. I cannot tell where Steloff gets into bed at night.

In a corner of the main room the kitchen alcove is portioned off by a delicately printed Hawaiian screen. On a large round table nearby are boxes of herb teas, fruits, nuts, grains, and dishes. Once Steloff offered to make dinner for me and a friend, an invitation we were delighted to accept because Steloff rarely extends herself in this way. She made an omelette, a salad of shredded carrots and cabbage, rice pudding, and dandelion root tea.

During the rice pudding we talked about the practice of reflexology — the art of massaging zones of the feet to assuage ills of the body. When my friend declared she had aching feet at the moment, Steloff volunteered immediately to treat them. She went into the bathroom, where hangs Steloff's reflexology degree amidst old fashioned chemises. Without bothering to close the door, she took off her dirndl skirt and donned soft white pyjamas and a long, cotton Japanese kimono. She let down her hair and emerged from the bathroom with a towel over her arm and a bottle of oil in one hand. She grinned mysteriously. I was so delighted by her transformation from businesswoman to masseuse that I took out my camera.

She pulled a stool close to my friend and set the oil elixir down beside her. She began to massage my friend's feet. Suddenly I noticed a light glowing around my friend's head, which I attempted to photograph. Later when I printed the negatives I was stunned to see vibrant rays of light curling like smoke around my friend's body. Steloff conjectured that the flaming aura was released energy, produced by her massaging the feet. From then on I believed in her reputation for having healing hands.

When we talk, usually Steloff and I sit down on the only two chairs available. Hers is a rocker which she bought years ago for $5. This chair, placed near the only lamp in the room, is her favorite place to read. I pull a low straight chair as close to her as possible so that, although she does most of the talking, she'll be able to hear me when I say something. The room is semi-dark. She folds her hands in her lap, holds her shoulders back proudly, and intently turns her eyes on me.

I lose myself in the white hair swirling around her face and reflect how this woman's body and soul went into the making of the Gotham Book Mart, how her life pulled together the heartfelt, often unspoken, needs of writers and readers. Each book on a Gotham shelf has a personal relationship with Steloff, as does every presentation, party, and lecture. She has put decades into tending them. Her body and spirit are worn and burnished from years of making choices and overcoming obstacles to maintain the shop's existence. The Gotham Book Mart and the life of Frances Steloff are so intertwined that it is impossible to see them separately.

She reaches over to the bookshelf, removes some books, and thrusts one in my lap. The title is **Saratoga Trunk.** Another book is handed over — **Conversations at Midnight.** Then another — **In This Our Time.** Also **Mein Kampf** and **Ulysses.** Intrigued, I open each of them. Each is a journal of hers, filled entirely in her hand. They are publishers' dummies, originally empty pages bound to show the format. What treasures, I thought, and how amusing! I pick up **Saratoga Trunk.** The illustration on the cover shows a young woman getting on a train with her suitcase. It could have been Frances Steloff once. I open it and begin to read, just as I have read other Steloff journals, letters, and published memoirs. (A chronological history of Frances Steloff and the Gotham Book Mart can be read in W.G. Rogers' **Wise Men Fish Here** (published in 1965, now out of print.) For detailed portraits of the many famous people and milestones, told in Steloff's own words, see the recently published **Journal of Modern Literature** (vol. 4, no. 4).

Her diary begins:

> **It was the last day in the year of 1887, the coldest winter anyone could remember, that I made my appearance. I had been told that I was born on New Year's Day, and not until I needed a birth certificate in order to get a passport did I discover the error. I had always thought New Year's Day the perfect day to begin life, and asked my aunt who was supposed to remember everything that ever happened in the family, if there might be some error in the registration, but all she could say was that they got the news on the first of the year and so I was always remembered as the New Year's baby . . .**

Steloff's statement that she **made an appearance** rather than **was born** reflects her belief that her spirit was given a body at that particular time by a particular set of parents. She does not believe that a person is born, i.e., created totally anew. The physical body is biologically prepared and can die, eventually disappearing into earth, but the spirit or soul never dies, having an eternal existence with comparatively brief earthly sojourns. Hence Steloff says **I made my appearance** in her curious, precise way.

Steloff was proud to be the first born in America of her Russian Jewish family. At the time of her birth the sun was in Capricorn, moon in Cancer and Gemini her ascendant. Her first memory is **standing against the wall in the kitchen, hands on hips, with my mother squatting before me clapping her hands to a tune that I might dance to. My next memory is in my aunt's house. There was great sorrow and tears while Mother** *slept* **in a long wooden box on the floor. I tried to awaken her. I was 3½ years old.**

Steloff's childhood forced her into independence at an early age. Besides the death of her mother, conditions were tough and very poor. She lived with two sisters and two brothers in rural Saratoga Springs, New York. In Winter their house was often freezing. The toilet was outside. They often had nothing to eat but root vegetables.

In order to have someone take care of the house and children while he worked away from home, the father quickly remarried. The couple continued to foster children, making conditions even harder. As a child, Steloff had the responsibility for chores concerning the animals, house, and caring for the new babies. Steloff bitterly says, **There never was a time when we didn't have babies, nor can I remember when we didn't have to wash diapers and prepare bottles. Babies were an annual event.** This is probably the best single reason why Steloff never had any babies of her own as an adult.

The pain of her childhood looms large in her memories. Her step-mother beat her and had harsh words for the slightest mishap. Yet, Steloff knows her step-mother unleashed her angers because she was powerless and isolated to do anything about the cold, hunger, or poverty of her brood, half of which was not hers. They all suffered. Many years later on a visit with her aged step-mother, Steloff noted the matted condition of her hair and decided to fill a basin with warm sudsy water and wash the hair. At the same time she spontaneously washed her step-mother's feet, as a welcome apology for all the resentment she stored up in those early years. It turned out to be the last time Steloff was to see her alive.

Frances' father was frequently away selling dry goods. Because
he was not there to bear the brunt of the daily anxiety and trouble,
he obviously became something of a relief figure for young Frances.
Of all in her childhood, she endows him with the most affection
and respect. She recalls the gentle care he gave his farm animals, for
instance, the way he would warm their food before feeding them in
Winter. She liked his spirit of reverence and sincerity. When he rose
at dawn, he started a fire, tended the cows, and said prayers. For
planting and harvest times he also had special prayers. At holidays
because there was no synagogue he conducted services for others
at an aunt's home. She says, **When he discussed the** *Talmud,* **he
poured out his heart without restraint. Everyone was refreshed and
uplifted. Some, with tears in their eyes, said he could move the
heart of a stone.**

Frances Steloff always loved the country and later, when she
was dwelling in the city, she would long to be among the flowers
(to her there is no such thing as *weed*) and animals, and lost a job
once because of seizing an opportunity to vacation in the country.
But as a child her only pleasure was picking berries in the pasture
while tending the cows. Life was an endless round of chores —
feeding the animals, sewing, shopping, cooking, raising vegetables,
selling flowers to the wealthy vacationers on the streets of Saratoga
Springs — which created in her a yearning to hop on a train and
get away from it all.

Before escaping, however, two ideas were firmly planted in her
mind. One occurred to her when she saw her pet calf slaughtered.
Shocked and horrified, she rebelled and henceforth refused to eat
meat. To this day grief clouds her face when she thinks of the
mother cow's expression and the calf's suffering. She is pained not
just by the imagined hurt to the animals but by her conviction
that the cruelty of slaughter, the agony of death at the hands of
men, enters the man and the food, thereby poisoning both. Therefore, to her, when we eat meat, we are eating the violence of man
and the pain of helpless victims. The evil becomes part of us and
is responsible for the continuing destruction we wreak upon others
and the world.

Steloff's second awakening concerned her innate love for books.
She experienced this first at her grandmother's house where there
was a pile of books on a marble-top table in the corner, each of

which seemed more thrilling than the other. Although sympathetic, her elders obliged her to leave them alone. In school she learned a rhyme which she never forgot: **Keep a watch on your words, my darling, for words are wonderful things.** Books were alive to her; her love for them burned inside her, like fuel.

When Steloff was 12½ years old a fairly prosperous couple who lived in Boston asked her father if she could live with them as a companion to the wife. Her father felt she should have the opportunity to do so. Thus, at last, leaving Saratoga, young Frances, in a photograph, looks like the girl on the cover of **Saratoga Trunk.** She wears a long dress, fashionable at the time. Her hair is pinned back with loose curls falling over her shoulders. Her eyes are large and appealing, her mouth full and turned down at the corners. Her usually bare feet are shod in boots. She stands wistfully alone.

While living with this couple, among other things Frances attended the seventh grade at school, had Dickens read to her, and met a Christian Scientist who took her to hear Mary Baker Eddy speak. But life became intolerable again, when the couple began to fight and the drunkenness of the wife obliged Frances to stay home from school to take care of her. One day when the woman beat her dog to death in a rage, it was too much to bear, and Frances ran away to New York City.

She was 15 years old and on her own in the big city. At first she was a governess and then she got a job at Loeser's Department Store in the corset department. In 1907 when Frances was 20, she met George Mischke, who managed Loeser's *old and rare book* department. When Steloff was chosen to help sell books at Christmas time, he gave her her first lesson in selling just as he would give her good advice in the years to come. He encouraged her to stay in the book department since she loved books so much. But after Christmas she was sent to the magazine department. Later Mischke got her a better position with books at Schulte's, where she says she learned the valuable lesson of **always leading a customer to the shelf where the book he is asking for should be, even if I had looked for the title five minutes before and knew we didn't have it, the idea being to get the customer looking at the subject in which he is interested.**

From then on Steloff stayed in the book business, steadily becoming more thoroughly experienced. She next worked at an excellent bookshop run by the McDevitt-Wilson's. There she frequently was put in charge by herself. She also had the privilege of taking books home to read after work. She describes how in those days fiction was published at one price but sold at less than the set price by department stores. To compete with this practice, Doubleday then opened up its own store. At McDevitt-Wilson's she also began to enjoy waiting on famous customers, being pleased when they would wait for her help. She found romance in bookselling. Everything about her life began to improve. She felt happier. For the first time the longing to be elsewhere ceased. She enjoyed city life.

She worked at Brentano's too. There she was responsible for their *troublesome booklets* and Mosher editions. She practiced writing strange difficult titles, such as **Rubaiyat of Omar Khayyam, Quattrocentisteria** by Maurice Hewlett, and **Virginibus Puerisque** by Robert Louis Stevenson. It was at Brentano's she met David Moss, the man later destined to be her husband.

For a brief period she went to Washington, D.C. as a buyer's assistant for Kahn & Son's. This large department store often bought slightly soiled or damaged books and sold them at a fraction of the published price. Otherwise, if a book didn't sell in a few months, it landed on the bargain table. Steloff protested because she liked to recommend books on a permanent shelf. She didn't like to have to sell them within a certain time limit nor be prevented from building up a good stock. When Steloff was able to do things her way in the Gotham Book Mart, she quickly became famous for saving everything. Her growing knack for buying old and rare books, as well as spotting first editions, resulted in her amassing valuable collections.

While in Washington Steloff went to **Bible** classes conducted by a Hebrew scholar. It was as though time now allowed her to continue her spiritual quest, which she sought to complement the practical demands of her life. The **Bible** to her had always been the first and foremost book. However, at the classes she met a woman who introduced her to the Browning Society where she absorbed the devotee's deep reverence for Browning's work, which seemed akin to her feeling for her father's religion. It impressed her that the hunger of people's souls was met by certain books. Spirit and books became united in her mind. Books of this nature henceforth were the most important to her.

She returned to New York and took a job with George Mischke's new shop. The first World War had begun and business was bad. When Mischke couldn't pay Steloff, she went back to Brentano's where she took care of the drama section.

In retrospect, Steloff's experiences in the book business came together at this point to produce the beginning of the Gotham Book Mart. One day in mid-December, 1919, she passed a *Space for Rent* sign in front of a brownstone set back between two remodeled buildings, three steps down from the sidewalk. She heard a voice within her say, **This is it. Go ahead. Take it.** Her spine burned. She paid attention to that fire within. It was like the way she felt when the **Bible** or Browning were read, only stronger.

It took courage to act upon that sign in front of the basement window. She was a woman and society didn't think it suitable for women to own businesses. She had very little money and rent for the room cost $75 a month. Her friends were not enthusiastic. Nobody believed in it except her. Yet if she hadn't acted, the Gotham would never have existed. The spine burning, the tingling excitement — that is the way the spirit within spoke — and she listened.

Rather than feeling foolish, Steloff felt extraordinarily fortunate to find an entire room even though the window was tiny. She put $10 down and took stock of her assets — a $100 Liberty Bond, almost $100 in cash, and a bookcase full of out-of-print theatre books. After paying a month's rent in advance, she moved in with 175 of her personally owned books. What to name the shop? She didn't want to use her own name. She liked *Book Mart,* and when a friend suggested *Gotham,* she thought that perfect. *Gotham* was an old English word meaning New York, which Washington Irving had used in his **Knickerbocker's History of New York.** Also, because Mr. Weyhe, who owned a successful art and book business, and had wanted Steloff to work for him, offered to give her a choice of art prints, she decided to call the shop **Gotham Art and Book Mart.** She was 33 years old when the Gotham was founded. Officially the Gotham's birthday is January 1, 1920.

George Mischke, once Steloff appeared intent on having her shop, advised, for one thing, that her first customer be a young person. Thus, Steloff describes how dismayed she was first to see an old man totter into her shop. She was relieved when he did not buy anything, since then he did not really count as a customer. The next person in her shop was a handsome young man who bought the most expensive book on her shelf. He was Glenn Hunter, at the time acting in Booth Tarkington's **Clarence** at the Hudson Theatre, eventually becoming a close friend. He inspired almost the entire cast of the play to come into the shop for books, which helped Steloff enormously. Not only was he an extraordinary customer, but also indicative of how important theatre people would be to the growth of the Gotham.

From the first Steloff took over the care of the Gotham like a mother does her baby. She never closed before midnight to allow for the theatre crowd to come. She took catalogs of American and British publishers to bed with her. And, in the morning she opened before nine. Working alone, she swept, shovelled snow, maintained the shelves, and kept the accounts. Sometimes she would be able to go out to eat if two or three friends took over for her at evening time.

She began to feel like a full-fledged businesswoman. An account with Baker & Taylor's gave her a wide range of choice from most publishers' books. Many customers came forward to help her in the first years, which made a big difference. Among early friends were associates of the Samuel French drama publishing company, and R.H. Burnside, stage director of the Hippodrome. The advertising manager of *The Billboard* gave the Gotham free advertising space as an experiment. And the representative from Scribner's offered to let Steloff order beautiful art books on consignment (an unheard of practice at the time), perhaps because he remembered that when Steloff worked at Brentano's she ordered 500 copies of Scribner's **Echoes of the War** by J.M. Barrie.

Keeping the shop open until after midnight, Steloff frequently had the company of a young friend, David Moss. His mother, with whom he lived, complained that their late hours seemed improper. At this juncture, too, occurred the death of Frances Steloff's beloved father. Such were the pressures on Frances Steloff when she and David Moss decided to marry. They were wed June 17, 1923. And to enable Moss to leave his former job, she gave him a half-interest in the Gotham Book Mart. The marriage did not work out and by the end of five years Steloff found herself almost overwhelmed by nervous exhaustion. This was the only event in her life that produced such a deep strain on her health that for the sake of peace she almost relinquished the Gotham Book Mart to Moss and considered opening an antique shop in Connecticut or taking courses at Columbia University. Even today she becomes rigid at the remembrance of this difficult period.

Business, however, expanded during this time. The Gotham Book Mart began to publish catalogs to develop a mail-order service. The bookshelves became crowded, especially after book-buying trips to Europe. When the lease was up on the present space, it was decided to relocate the Gotham Book Mart in larger quarters at 51 West 47th Street. In the same block other book stores competed for attention.

Steloff was amply prepared for the rigors of business by the hardships of her childhood. From the first she did most of the work alone. In later years when she could afford some assistance, she made sure her shop was run carefully and efficiently. Perhaps because she was a woman she tried doubly hard to maintain her standards, even acquiring a reputation for being frank and demanding. One of her iron principles involved serving her customers. She felt it was unpardonable to be out of a book that they would expect to find in her shop. If someone wanted a book that she didn't have, she called all the stores in town until she found a copy, which she would then deliver before the day was done. Or she would call up the publisher. If a book was out of print, she would advertise for it at no cost to the customer. Her customers were her pride and joy and nothing pleased her more than to have them rely on her. Her efforts made an impact on people and they came back.

Furthermore, Steloff never compromised on the types of books she offered for sale. She did not cater to the mass market by stocking *best-sellers,* detective stories, or science fiction. Nor did she specialize only in elegant rare books whose financial value lay in the fact that their authors were deceased. Barratt Clark in a letter best expressed her intentions: **I think you have always preferred to sell a $2.00 book of poems that would bring the author 20¢ in royalties, to making ten times that amount on the sale of the work of a deceased writer.** Her commitment to sell the best living literature extended to the books published in Paris by the expatriate generation, e.g., Gertrude Stein's Plain Editions, Harry and Caresse Crosby's beautiful Black Sun Press books, and Jack Kahane's Obelisk

Press which brought out controversial works, such as **Tropic of Cancer** by Henry Miller and **Lady Chatterley's Lover** by D. H. Lawrence. She opposed the taxing of books because she firmly believed in their cultural value to society. She stocked books that were written by highly respected practitioners of the word, as well as unknown writers whom either she or her author customers recognized as having an important way of saying something. The wonderful thing is that she survived in a materialistic era.

In 1930 Steloff was at last divorced. She raised the cash to buy out Moss' share of the Gotham Book Mart, and once again her destiny was one with the Gotham Book Mart's. The tension of negotiations plus the current economic depression left her weak, however, and for a few weekends she sought refuge at a rest home in Connecticut.

There she heard of Dr. Emmet Fox, whom she later would describe as introducing her to the kindergarten of spiritual life. He was for her the beginning of an exploration into many philosophies that have refined her beliefs to their present point. On the walls of the home had been posted brief messages of encouragement by him. The nurse said he was speaking in the ballroom of the Astor Hotel and that she would take Steloff. She learned later that he was part of the Church of the Healing Christ, which would have repelled her if she had known at the time she went to the lecture. She was disappointed in Fox's first talk but for two years continued to attend his weekly lectures.

Her strong belief in vegetarianism acquired a more spiritual foundation as she progressed. She says, *Thou shalt not kill* **applies to animals as well as humans and we have no right to retard their evolution. How can we ever hope to escape war while we shed their blood, creating more fear and pain in this sorrowful world?** Once when Steloff heard that Katharine Anne Porter was to have an operation, she persuaded her to read some books and make some changes in her diet. Katharine Anne Porter did not have the operation.

Steloff's inner cravings took her down many spiritual paths. She never accepted any *one* philosophy but feels that all contributed to her knowledge as a whole. When Dr. Fox went on vacation, she then went to a Theosophical meeting, where she learned extensively about reincarnation and karma and studied the **Bhagavad Gita.**

One of her favorite quotes was Socrates' **Education is drawing out the intelligence within.** She became a friend of the Vedanta Society and was an early student of Ouspensky's and Gurdjieff's philosophy before their ideas spread rapidly around the country and Europe. When Steloff first heard Joel Goldsmith lecture she was immediately impressed with him and invited him to speak at the Gotham. When she saw that he printed his work by mimeograph machine, she found a publisher to put out real books. Now his books fill several shelves in her alcove. She also closely studied the work of Rudolf Steiner and Lama Govinda. Steloff comments, **I was destined to be inspired by these people. It was not accidental. It was as if the hound of heaven just rounded me up and sent me to these places.**

Steloff began to feel she had a calling to help people in search of truth and to specialize in books on religion. Prior to then, she had avoided such books because in the early days when she worked at Brentano's the religious department was where customers, wearing sandals, strange turbans, meaningful jewelry, and flowing batiks congregated and talked a long time. Other clerks made fun of them, and so Steloff thought it best to avoid occult books. When one would come in she would put it under the table with other undesirable categories that she wouldn't give shelf room. **One day,** she says, **a big broad Negro came in and asked for** *The Secret Doctrine* **by Madame Blavatsky. I asked him why he came in for that book when Brentano's was on the corner and an occult shop close by. He answered that he happened to think of it passing my window.** After that omen she gave one shelf in the rear to the occult books most frequently called for. Now those books have an entire alcove and are crowding into other areas. One of Steloff's fervent desires was to produce a very fine catalog, which distinguished all the religions in the world and the books about them. (She produced one catalog of religious and mystical philosophy books, which, though not fully satisfactory to her, is still better than anything available.) Steloff liked the customers that those books attracted. They have been serious and sincere. **I have been able to help them by just directing them to the group it seemed they would find most helpful.** Now that the audience for esoteric religious and philosophical books has increased enormously shows how Steloff was intuitively ahead of her time. This has been her most rewarding experience.

For Steloff all too often the possibility loomed of losing her shop. One such time was after 25 years of business. The superintendent came in and announced that a new landlord was taking over her building as well as the three adjacent ones to put up a new building. Shortly thereafter the new owner sent notice that he would need her space for his own use. Steloff searched for another site nearby. Because she refused to start from scratch again in a new neighborhood, she felt that she would be forced to end her business. Mitchell Kennerly, a publisher and president of the now Parke Bernet Galleries who frequented the Gotham, heard her situation and offered to help. When she told him that a few doors down at 41 West 47th Street the building was owned by Columbia University but occupied by an antique shop, he wanted Steloff to buy the building. She did not believe the lot was for sale and even if it was she couldn't conceive of buying it, when just paying her rent was difficult enough. To this day Steloff does not know who then was instrumental in Columbia University's seemingly miraculous decision to allow Steloff to purchase the building for 25% down payment at the 1913 assessment with quarterly payments. Although it was hard for her to raise the down payment, and many advised her against taking on the responsibility of a building, she vowed not to abandon the Gotham Book Mart nor to disappoint those who had loved it for so many years. Incidents such as this confirmed her belief over the years that just as she put her life in service to her customers, the book lovers, so she received in full their aid at crucial times. **Nothing's wasted,** she quips.

> In her words: **Devotion to work is a sure way to form a partnership with God. We do not know the limits of endeavor, but while we are doing a better job without, we are building a better person within. Achievement becomes nourishment for the soul, which people who work grudgingly never discover. I believe that the best things that ever happened to me came because I loved my work. When you have devotion to work, and you can pass the tests, it will reward you in kind. The right people will notice. The fruits of your labor will come back to you.**

But at the time she struggled with her difficulties, she had no idea what the outcome would be. She learned that the more storms she endured with the Gotham, the more determined she was to hold on to it. Every set-back wove new threads into the cloth that bound them. Truly, every day at the Gotham was a spiritual challenge.

The people, her customers, were the touchstones through which her understanding of life and her self was refined and purified. With her customers she always had the attitude of listening for what they wanted. She would get the books they wanted, as she did for the Truth-seekers. Filling the needs of customers also led to the inclusion of the literary magazines, for which the Gotham Book Mart has always been famous. The literary magazines had art sections, such as in *Broom,* where the works of many modern artists (Picasso, Gris, Matisse, Lipschitz, Man Ray) were reproduced for the first time. She took in the most distinguished as well as the most bohemian productions. Steloff says: **Gradually as editors and writers began urging the magazines on us, we took more and more of the strictly avant-garde. Perhaps it would be more flattering to believe that we were prophets about the great new writers who were then emerging in these little reviews; but on the contrary, I was led step by step by opportunities, and simply responded to the needs and requests for an outlet.**

She took on Titus' *This Quarter,* T. S. Eliot's *Criterion,* Cyril Connelly's *Horizon.* Taking on *transition,* which included the most experimental writers, especially James Joyce, led to hundreds of people coming into the shop hungry for every issue. She took on Whit Burnett and Martha Foley's *Story,* published in Vienna, and soon it became the most important magazine devoted to the short story, as well as the first to offer prizes to new and unknown writers. These magazines at the time had no distribution, nor is the situation much better now. Steloff says editors of these magazines have always acted as if their very life depended on getting their little mags published. In early magazines were contributions by E.E. Cummings, William Carlos Williams, Ezra Pound, Ernest Hemingway, who were then as unknown as the little magazines in which they appeared. The Gotham Book Mart was perhaps the only place in the country where you could get such a complete collection of the magazines. Authors began to depend on them for the dispersion of their work and for a little extra money for food and rent.

Publishers and readers eventually realized the enormous value of magazines in the development of new writers, for many of the best writers first appeared in the unheralded pages of the magazines.

Steloff treated customers as a mother does her children, also as if they had something to teach her (which wise parents know children do). She says, **To be sure you have the proper spirit, you cannot be selfish toward others, nor manipulating.** One way she sought to assist her customers was by bringing out lists of the books of avant-garde authors in brochures which came to be called *GBM Currents.* These were so well received that she also published fuller catalogs on first editions or a specific author, such as Gertrude Stein. One catalog was titled *The Book-Collectors' Odyssey* or *Travels in the Realms of Gold.* For the shop's 20th anniversary in 1940 she planned a really special catalog. With typical genius she asked the writers themselves to introduce their favorite author's books in the catalog. This also saved her from having to make a direct sales pitch, which she always abhorred.

James Laughlin, of *New Directions,* said in a review of a catalog:

> **In this catalog they (Frances Steloff and her assistant, Key Steele) have made more than a list of their wares; it is a bibliography of the cream of contemporary literature. Entrance is by merit only — not by canned sales and publishers' blurbs. These books were written by people who think that writing is something more than a way to make a living. Ezra Pound has hardly made as much money in a lifetime as your broker makes in a year. Henry Miller can tell you what it feels like to be so hungry you don't dare try to eat. The Pulitzer committee . . . won't feel at home here . . . Some of these books were written in blood. It is a taste you may never forget.**

The *Currents* and the catalogs are literary gems, well worth poring through. Nothing else exists like them; they are now collectors' items. Besides, each has the Steloff touch of an inspiring quotation such as this one from Krishnamurti:

> **The fact is that life is like the river: endlessly moving on, ever seeking, exploring, pushing, over-flowing its banks, penetrating every crevice with its water. But, you see, the mind won't allow that to**

> **happen itself. The mind sees that it is dangerous, risky . . . so it builds a wall around itself . . . a mind which is seeking permanency soon stagnates; like that pool along the river, it is soon full of corruption, decay. Only the mind which has no walls, no foothold, no barrier, no resting place, which is moving completely with life, timelessly pushing on, exploring, exploding — only such a mind can be happy, eternally new, because it is creative in itself.**

The *We Moderns* catalog, the 1940 anniversary issue, received a flood of praises from people in letters and reviews and newspaper articles around the country. It was considered a superlative document on modern authors, as well as a new and wonderful way to sell books. Steloff says, **It marked a turning point in the history of the GBM. It seemed as if the work and struggle of twenty years had suddenly reached fruition. It put the GBM on the literary map.**

Frances Steloff also undertook the sponsoring of writers she believed needed help. Thus, the Gotham came to be called a writers' bookshop, not only because the best of modern literature could be found there, but also because of the many ways it went to battle for writers — the court trials, the publication parties, the sub-rosa loans. Steloff went even further and published certain works under the GBM imprint. One was **Vertical,** edited by Eugene Jolas and publicized as **new spiritual literature for a materialistic 20th century.** Others were the D.H. Lawrence/Bertrand Russell letters, ed. by Harry T. Moore; poems by Gertrude Stein and Wallace Stevens.

Steloff pressured publishers about reprinting desirable authors' works which were out-of-print. For instance, she was instrumental in getting Swami Muktananda's book, **Guru,** and Goldsmith's **The Mystical I,** taken on by Harper & Row. Harper & Row afterwards wrote letters of gratitude to Steloff for steering them their way. Steloff's correspondence is huge and much of it contains a bit of the formidable forthrightness for which she is well-known. Here is an exchange between Steloff and Bennett Cerf, the president of Random House; the matter at hand is William Faulkner's **Absalom, Absalom.**

Dear Bennett:

This is to serve notice that you will not have peace or rest until you promise to reprint **Absalom, Absalom.** We have been advertising for many months without receiving a single quotation. Now at last I get the enclosed. A quotation from a dealer offering it at $74.25.

I called the guy up just to see if he was serious, and sure enough the 25¢ is for postage and insurance, he explains, rare books must be insured. The last copy we sold for $20.00 and I thought we were robbing the poor customer, but there is no other way to lay hands on this title.

We have a poor student in Germany who made great sacrifices to get $7.50 to us; about six months ago we thought we could supply one at that price. And so we keep on searching without success. It is as you must know the most important of all Faulkner titles, and Faulkner has been on the up and up for the last two years.

Will you not take my word for it that it will be the best selling title in the Modern Library for a very long time. I had hoped to avoid annoying you and thought I would extract a promise from Saxe (Commins) but he passed the buck.

With love and Easter greetings.

Always,
(signed) Frances

Dear Frances:

Thanks for your note about **Absalom, Absalom,** and I am impressed to see a price of $74.25 quoted for a copy thereof.

We most certainly are going to put this book in the Modern Library, but that won't be until the Fall of 1951. This Fall we are doing **Light In August** in the Modern Library. We are also doing a volume of Faulkner's collected short stories as a Random House

publication. Eventually, every line that Faulkner has
ever written will be back in print.

In short, my dear, I ask you only to keep your
pants on, which is certainly something I wouldn't
have told a girl twenty years ago. Time marches on,
God damn it.

> Love,
> (signed) Bennett

Dear Bennett:

Thanks for your prompt reply, but am I satisfied?
I should say not.

Why do you publish **Light in August** which is available from New Directions ahead of **Absalom, Absalom**
which is scarcer than hen's teeth, and far more in
demand because it is his best title.

I never could understand why publishers behave the
way they do, but you used to be different. I wish I
had the time to make up a list of the Sins of publishers.

> Love as usual,
> (signed) Frances

Recently as reported in *The New York Times* a person published
two volumes of J.D. Salinger's stories without Salinger's permission
or knowledge. When the person tried to sell them to the Gotham
Book Mart, the Gotham refused to take the volumes and alerted
Salinger to what was happening. In such a way the GBM protected
its authors, rather than use them commercially. I witnessed another
example of support once when I was visiting with Steloff, and an
old man came in with some of his deceased brother's books. He was
forced to sell them because of his impoverished condition, and as
he talked, be began to cry. Steloff instantly said she would help him.
She served her friends with respect and dignity. When Caresse Crosby,
a woman Steloff admired a great deal, died, she coordinated a
memorial meeting for her, for which many of her famous friends,
including Buckminster Fuller, Anais Nin, and Kay Boyle wrote
memorial contributions.

One of Frances Steloff's most famous accomplishments was to launch the James Joyce Society, which was the result again of following the suggestions of customers and filling their needs. The Gotham had always been a major source for Joyce's work, especially in the magazines. Students often came in, asking questions which Steloff couldn't answer, although she knew who the authorities on Joyce's work were. She decided to bring them together in a study group. She spoke to John Slocum, who had one of the finest collections of Joyceana in the world, Professor William Tindall and his assistant, James Gilvarry, the actor Roland von Weber who played the lead rold in **Exiles,** and Ben Huebsch who first published Joyce in America. Instead of a study group it became the James Joyce Society, founded in 1947 at the Gotham Book Mart, six years after the death of Joyce.

Steloff has always personally organized the meetings and fussed over the arrangement of chairs and wine. Then when everyone arrives, she glows with pleasure and embraces friends. Distinguished speakers have addressed the Society, including Padraic Colum, Thornton Wilder, Joseph Campbell, Stephen Joyce, Leon Edel, and Irish Joycean scholars. Mary Ellen Bute, film director and producer of *Passages from Finnegan's Wake,* dedicated the script to Steloff for her 75th birthday, as a testament to all that the GBM had done to make possible research by admirers and scholars of Joyce. Steloff went still further and gave Columbia University $10,000 for a fund in honor of Professor Tindall, Mary and Padraic Colum for continued study and research on Joyce. This gesture, I am sure, is one of many little known acts in keeping with Frances Steloff's commitment.

Another now famous literary institution are the GBM parties which were held in a garden before the days of the Gallery. The practice had its origin when the Gotham was located at 51 W. 47th Street. There was a backyard and a portable garage which was used as a stockroom, and one day when Sam Putnam, editor of *The New Review*, asked if he could give a lecture back there, Steloff cleaned it up and draped a velvet curtain over an old ice box for the rostrum. There a lecture series on contemporary French writers, followed by a symposium for small literary magazine editors, inaugurated many enchanting parties. People liked being outdoors where they could open their collars, smoke and relax. Steloff brought in flowers and plants, had bookstalls built exactly like the ones along the Seine in Paris. As artists and writers felt the benefits of gathering for lectures and parties, they became a GBM tradition. Steloff once joked that her favorite sport at the time was catching caterpillars on the shrubs and weeding the flower beds.

Wherever Steloff went she always peddled books. When authors such as Allen Ginsberg or Dylan Thomas were giving a lecture she would arrive with shopping bags or cartons of books and sell them herself. At the Poetry Center she is a tradition, every week sitting behind a booth laden with fresh, aromatic books, arranged as nicely as a dinner party setting. She was the only one given such authority and has been at the Poetry Center ever since William Carlos Williams was the first to read there. The Poetry Center would not be the same without the Gotham Book Mart's presence.

In 1968, after 48 years of running the GBM, Steloff sold the shop to Andreas Brown, a young bibliophile and rare bookman from California. In their agreement she has remained as active consultant. Brown has his own ideas for the shop, which inevitably will make it not quite the same intimate place. Business has flourished and the fame of the GBM has continued to spread in the past decade. More catalogs and books have been issued. Early in 1975 Brown negotiated the sale of 65% of GBM's holdings in order to pave the way for another relocation to larger quarters. Steloff sees the move as another miracle in the life of the Gotham.

Since the sale to Brown, Frances Steloff has committed herself to sorting the mountain of papers, photographs, and memorabilia that have accumulated over half a century. A dozen crates of correspondence were donated to the New York Public Library. She has returned to her own writing. Following are some excerpts, which reveal her special sensibility, from her portraits of GBM's closest friends and literary legends.

EDITH SITWELL

One day in 1948, Charles came in and announced that Edith Sitwell and her brother Osbert were coming to America for a series of readings. In the same breath he asked, **Why don't you have a tea for her?**

Oh, said I, **She would have far more important engagements than coming here for tea.**

But Charles insisted. **She'd love it, and why don't you invite her?**

I did and back came this letter:

> The Sesame Club
> 49 Grosvenor Street
> London W. 1.

21 September: 1948
Dear Miss Steloff:

What a charming letter of welcome and invitation! . . .

My brother Osbert will be just as delighted as I am, when I show him your letter. He is at this moment at his house in Italy. It is so very charming of you to ask us . . .

We both think a day *after* a Reading is better than the day before a Reading, because of our voices. And for the same reason intensified, we never do anything on the actual day of our Reading. How exciting this is for us!

You, personally, and the Gotham Book Mart, are legends in our lives. I will think about the out-of-print works, about which you write so kindly . . .

> With many thanks
> yours sincerely
> Edith Sitwell

I will bring over my book on Shakespeare for you personally. It will be one of the only copies extant, as it will not yet have appeared in England.

The party for the Sitwells, in which their publishers, the Vanguard Press, collaborated, was a party to end all parties. The date was November 19, 1948. Not only everyone who was invited came, but everyone brought a friend. *Life* heard about it, and came to take pictures which have often been reprinted in books and magazines. There were so many people in the shop that I couldn't make my way from the tea table to the alcove where Miss Sitwell sat — pining for a cup of tea.

The next morning Winthrop Palmer called up and said, **Frances, you are the most famous hostess in New York.**

Bennett Cerf gave a lively account of the party in his column *Trade Winds* in the *Saturday Review of Literature* of December 11, 1948:

The Gotham Book Mart's do for Sir Osbert and Dr. Edith Sitwell brought out the darndest assortment of celebrities, freaks, refugees from Park Lane, and the lifted-pinkie set since the famous party for Joan *Cradle-of-the-Deep* **Lowell aboard the Ile de France in 1929. Wystan Auden, Tennessee Williams, William Saroyan, Jim Farrell, Carl Van Vechten, Marianne Moore, Stephen Spender, William Carlos Williams, Lincoln Kirstein, and Bill Benet were ogled and fought over like movie stars in front of the Hampshire House. One bearded gent wore a red velvet smoking jacket and looked disdainful. Another sported a Navajo Indian robe and looked dirty. The inevitable** *Life* **photographers knocked glasses out of hands of distinguished guests and blandly shooed Hostess Frances Steloff out of her own back office. That I managed to reach the side of Dr. Edith myself was a tribute to the all-American interference provided by Mary McGrory of the** *Washington Star*

who neatly took out the last apparition with a swivel-hipped feint and an astonished, My God, I think that was Oscar Wilde!

Dr. Edith was taking the commotion in stride. *As I say in my lectures, I don't like talent,* **she was telling one poet.** *I prefer power and conviction. I hear you were funny once in Liverpool,* **I shouted over the din.** *Would you tell me the details?* **Dr. Edith beamed . . . and said,** *Sit down here with me. The incident to which you refer occurred when I was discussing the poetry of D.H. Lawrence. I said it was* soft, wooly, and hot like a Jaeger sweater. *I thought Lawrence would have a fit but he didn't. The Jaegers, however, did. They informed me indignantly that their sweaters were indeed soft and wooly, but never hot, due to their* special system of slow conductivity.

HENRY MILLER

The first time I met Henry Miller was when he came in to ask how his little magazines, *The Booster* and *Delta*, were selling. This was in the late thirties. The next thing I knew, I got a letter from him in Paris. It was dated April 30, 1939.

Dear Miss Steloff:

I write to inquire if you would be interested in buying some first editions of **Tropic of Cancer** and **Black Spring** — I have about 20 of the first and 15 of the second left. If you would take the whole lot off my hands, I would let you have them for $350.00 — that is, $10. a piece.

I replied at once: **I wish we could take over all of** *Tropic of Cancer* **and** *Black Spring* **but cannot make the investment especially with the problem of getting**

them here. However, if you can see your way clear
and cannot do better elsewhere, we will send you
$200 for the lot. Miller accepted our offer in a
cable in which he said that he was leaving soon
for Greece.

After he got back to New York, he often dropped by
the bookstore, especially since there was a French
restaurant next door, Chez Maurice, and he liked the
French cuisine. We used to argue about how to help
artists and writers. Miller thought they should be
supported by the government and I said that perhaps
we would all like to be writers and artists if we
didn't have to earn a living. We quarreled violently,
and once he threatened never to come into the shop
again.

I had an idea for a fund from which writers and
artists could borrow without interest and without a
time limit. In those days there were hardly any
grants, and it took months to get them. I remembered how helpful the Hebrew Free Loan Society
had been in 1920 when I started the shop. I could
borrow a hundred dollars without interest and pay
it back in small weekly installments. But I was
strongly opposed to giving people money outright.
I thought it should be paid back, among other
reasons so that it could be loaned to others who
needed it.

In November 1940, letters went out to a group of
people asking them to come to Chez Maurice as
guests of the Gotham Book Mart to discuss the
best means of giving immediate assistance to writers.
We are not asking for money at this meeting, the
letter said, but believe that we have some good
ideas and would welcome your opinion. The letter
went to W.H. Auden, Maria Jolas, Paul Rosenfeld,
Genevieve Taggard, Kenneth Patchen, Henry Miller,

George Barker and a few others. As it turned out, we did collect some money that evening — but instead of keeping it as the beginning of the Writers' Emergency Fund, we wound up by distributing it then and there. (We had made the mistake of inviting the poor poets.)

H. L. MENCKEN

H. L. Mencken's first book was a volume of poetry, **Ventures into Verse,** written in his youth, and the time came when he was ashamed of it. He used to buy and destroy all the copies he could find. We managed to find a few and turned them over to Mencken — until we found that they were to be destroyed. Then we found a copy with marginal notations that had been made by Mencken himself. One of them read, **I wrote this when I was Kipling-mad.** When Mencken heard that we had it, he offered to give us $2000 worth of advertising in *The American Mercury* in return for the book. We refused to let him get his hands on it — though he came in several times to try to persuade us. We finally sold the book to a collector. Mencken, however, continued to come in. One day he arrived with Theodore Dreiser. They were both in a happy mood, as if they had had a few extra beers, and discovering their own books, began autographing them. When they had finished with their own, they started autographing other books. One of them was a pulpit **Bible** in which Dreiser signed as his disciple, or vice versa — I cannot remember.

MARIANNE MOORE

Marianne Moore came in with her mother on one of her early visits. She was carrying a black net bag full of magazines and books that she wanted to dispose of. As we were taking them out, I mentioned that I could give her half of the publishers' prices. Hearing this, her mother scolded, **Now, Marianne, those books were given to you and you are not supposed to take any money for them!** I thought I'd better drop the subject until Marianne came in alone.

At that time Marianne's publisher was Macmillan. Every year they remaindered some of their overstock, and one year they had some wonderful titles for us that included 200 copies of **Collected Poems** by Marianne Moore. I said I'd take them all. When Marianne Moore heard that I had bought all the remaindered copies, she came in to see me. She said that they had some typographical errors, and asked if I would mind if she came in whenever she had time and corrected them.

Of course, nothing could have been sweeter for us, so we made a little corner for her and she came in two or three times a week to make the corrections. Well, we sold those books at the publisher's price of $2, instead of $1 as I had planned, and by the time they were gone I would have paid $25 each to get them back.

Marianne's funeral, held in the very old church in Brooklyn that she had attended for more than 30 years, was as informal as she had wished it to be. She had chosen the music, and one of the prayers was the one she composed for her mother's funeral in 1947. The only words on the cover of the blue booklet commemorating the service were:

**Beauty is everlasting
and dust is for a time.**

As a tribute to Frances Steloff, Sam Putnam wrote the following
in his introduction to the *We Moderns* catalog:

> **If its (the Gotham Book Mart's) success has been
> somewhat phenomenal, and those in the trade
> will assure you that it has been, this has been
> due to the fact that Frances Steloff, the Gotham's
> founder, was at once so finely attuned to the
> literary age in which she lived, so catholic in her
> range of sympathies in an era that was, when all
> is said, one of questings and wholesale documen-
> tation, and so unflinchingly courageous from both
> a financial and an esthetic point of view . . . the
> Gotham was a good literary free-for-all, the only
> requirement being that the writer must be of his
> time and at least trying desperately hard to say
> something to his time. Whether they survived or
> not, the young writer and the young editor have
> reason to be grateful to Frances Steloff and to
> the Gotham for having given them a fighting
> chance. After all, what more could one ask for
> in an age in which the salesmanager is, commonly,
> the final arbiter of literary destinies?**

Thus the Gotham Book Mart became the place where literary
people found a comfortable, protective, illuminating haven. The
parties, lectures, James Joyce Society, and catalogs are all ways
in which Steloff created an atmosphere that kindled warmth and
friendship. Above all, her efforts brought writers and readers and
publishers and reviewers, anyone involved with books, into the
shop, buying books and spreading the good word. Many are grateful
to Steloff but typically none are more grateful than Steloff is to
the people who cared. Her achievements became the joys which
offset the hardships. To assess her success it is necessary to keep in
mind that Steloff did the menial work as well as the more exciting.
She took care of printing and mailing invitations, telephone calls,
refreshments in addition to the selling of books. She said once,
**There is no possibility of being happy without making a contribu-
tion.** And when CBS t.v. came to film a documentary with

Salvador Dali at the Gotham, Steloff appeared in three different aprons, swept the floors, and passed hors d'oeuvres herself, a living symbol of her attitude, even though she was a celebrity herself.

Steloff at 88 is still active in the bookshop, just pausing to joyfully reminisce now and then with friends. In the mornings when she awakes she meditates and does yoga exercises on a mat. After feeding herself and the cats, she goes down to be with the books and the many people who come to the shop. Almost every night of the week she is invited to parties, dinners, ceremonies, operas, dances, films, lectures with the most important literary men and women of our time. Recently the Author's Guild, the American Poetry Society, the State of New York, and the National Institute of Arts and Letters honored her. But she much prefers, indeed, to be among the books and the people who want them, the ones waiting in the shop, coming and going, the world feeding on books.

Steloff's intuition, cultivated over the years, played a large role in her life accomplishment. She says, **Booksellers do not necessarily read all the books they promote; they spark them and create a climate wherein birds of a feather may flock together.** She specialized in knowing the contents of a book and the nature of its author without reading it. She has a genius for putting into the hands of a customer the book he or she needs at the moment, although the person may not know it yet. Her intuition, gentleness and common sense have been her strengths, although Steloff always felt inferior in business for lack of financial expertise, and in literature and philosophy for inability to pass critical judgement. Yet she knew books and people by instinct better than some scholars and critics.

She is a striking example of a human being not dominated by intellectual qualities, but one whose intuition controls the intellect. She possesses gifts that have been sorely lacking in technological corporation man, and which many feel have been undeveloped in human beings generally, but which hold promise for the future. As a woman, by being able to be soft and nurturing as well as forceful and pioneering, by never losing her sensitivity nor her sense, she maintained, in psychological terms, a sound androgynous balance.

Steloff's present life is an incarnation of her spirit. She hopes to reach a karma-less state, so that when she enters her next stage she will be free of past limitations. In this life she has tried to be a force and movement toward the Good. Once when I was having a difficult time with a business friend, Steloff gripped my arms and said, **Suffer it to be so now.** I looked at her mutely and felt her eyes bore into mine. **You are being tested. You must clear your feelings. Only then will you receive guidance.** She urged me to set my sights on the larger issues.

The key to Steloff's success lies in her power to pay attention to that *hound of heaven* seizing her in its grip to do her duty. **Those who cannot believe in the invisible will never do the impossible,** she said, after spending a lifetime learning the proof.

Anaïs Nin

Witch of Words

My purpose here is to focus on the young Anais Nin in the process of becoming a writer, primarily before the period covered by Nin's **Diary, Volume I.** Nin has proved that she was always a writer, despite the conflicts of her life and the views of parents, friends, psychoanalysts, and critics. It is well known that Anais Nin at the age of 11 began keeping a diary as a long letter to the father from whom she was separated. But the first published **Diary — Volume I —** begins when the author is 28 years old in 1931.

By that time stories by Nin had been published in various literary, mostly French, publications as well as her first book, **D.H. Lawrence: An Unprofessional Study.** She was working on other pieces, a novel at least, stories that would ultimately appear in **Under a Glass Bell,** and the prose-poem, **House of Incest.** Prior to these published works the author wrote other novels and stories, which have never been published, although some are available for study at the Library of Northwestern University.

The unpublished material in the Library's Special Collections Department is especially significant for showing the progress of Anais Nin's writing. Reading through her novels, beginning with the first, written in her teens, is a fascinating trip into the development of a writer. The heretofore unknown stories and the early drafts of **House of Incest** show Nin's techniques of creation, her refinement of words. Her early, always passionate concerns can be observed as they develop and change as she lives and writes. Knowledge of Anais Nin's early work enlarges awareness of the creative process; it is like watching seeds grow and become many different flowers. One becomes more intimately acquainted with the personage of Anais Nin.

For all writers, writing is a brave act. It is especially difficult when the writer is young, for then she is searching for her own voice, seeking a comfortable framework, comparing herself to other masters, and justifying time spent at this activity to others. Creative-writing teachers have their own ideas about what should be written and are often not so acute in perceiving the student's uniqueness. The English novel is usually taken as the standard for demonstrating literary method. Writers also face rejection slips and so building confidence becomes an endurance test. Anais Nin's writing, remarkably, is consistently strong and deft. Her voice is assured. She is serious with intellectual objectivity and depth. In using language she can be cool, with high aesthetic standards, as well as profusely ardent. One of her strengths is that from the beginning she did not hide herself behind words but sought to express herself as openly as possible. She is a self-taught writer, and, as she grew, she found ways to strengthen the sound of her inner voice.

Indeed, Anais Nin can be described as a witch of words. Very early she sensed the magical power of words to produce states of being, such as ecstasy, languor or dread. Her ambition was to transform the ugly realities of life into beauty, as the beast in fairy tales becomes the handsome prince after achieving a certain wisdom. She desired to distill the pure from the dross, and writing was her charm. Through writing she can inhabit other worlds for herself. Writing is a drug of the imagination. It casts spells on others, putting them into new worlds with her. Dreams can be lived out. The magic of words has also a healing effect. By writing she can examine her wounds privately and confront all the loose ends of her daily life, the unspoken but very present psychological currents. The act of creation itself is a balm, a tonic. The work of art is the witch's marvelous gift to the world. It is created from intense living and contemplation. Life itself is the witch's cauldron. The writing witch uses words to transform, heal, and teach wisdom. Her fresh awarenesses about the meaning of life for men and women have the capacity to change their lives.

Another way Anais Nin casts a magic spell is her ability to influence others by wishing them to be busy at their own creations. Countless people have testified to having experienced this. She inspires people to make creativity a way of life in the sense that the Balinese mean it when they say, *Art is doing anything well.*

I first discovered the work of Anais Nin after several discouraging years of sending my writing around to magazines and receiving rejections. This also corresponded with my marriage to a writer and the birth of two children. I had also been so conditioned by an academic education in literary criticism that I was unable to accept the diary form as literature. Thus, when I first saw Nin's books on the shelf, I had a closed mind toward the **Diary** and I surmised the novels were too avant-garde. Rather staidly I settled for the book of stories, **Under a Glass Bell.** That book was a powerful introduction.

Soon afterwards I became involved with a feminist art group which focused on women's condition in society. As I conducted my own reexamination of womanhood, I read all of Anais Nin's **Diaries.** She became for me the most important representative of the questing female writer. When I was 32 years old I could read and identify with her struggles in her thirties to write her books and achieve recognition. Because she is generous I visited her, exchanged letters, held a weekend symposium for her, and produced a book on that radiant event. I read and reread her books, collected publishers' first editions and the rare books which she typeset and printed by hand. She confirmed my youthful passion for writing and literature because she conquered hopelessness herself. She is dedicated to the fully realized personal self. She plunges into the chaotic sea of intimate, responsible relationships with compassion and genuine concern. With the tools of psychoanalysis and her own sensitive inner radar system she probed her actions and the unconscious powers behind them. In communication with the world she strove for tender solicitude among people as well as independence, liberty and integration of the self. Her life is epic and evanescent; her contemplation of it is the exploration, embodied by the art of her books.

In her books I was attracted, like many others, to her treatment of personal relationships. Separation from the father (in my case it was by divorce) created a longing for his love and respect. Nin's fascination for June in **Diary I** expressed the nature of love for a woman I felt too. In Nin's describing her experiences with Henry Miller, I saw the story of my husband and me when we first met, both fiery about writing, independent but coming together for the sparking of each other that could only happen in rare communion. In her renderings of people's sensibilities as she perceived them, Nin indirectly bestowed the gift of understanding to others again and again.

From her earliest diary entries Anais Nin was concerned with the personal details that are concealed from outward appearances by necessity or fear of reprisal and the real nature of life. When she was 11 years old, she wrote:

> **Today I have nothing to tell so I will chat with my**
> **diary, or rather, my confidant, for I write here many**
> **things I never tell anyone and that nobody knows.**
> **Let us begin: Today when I opened a book at hazard**
> **I read: Life is only a sad reality. Is it true?**

Photographs of the young Anais show a graceful, wistful girl. She has flowers in her hair and writes pensively. She began her diary-keeping on the boat to America and early entries contain passages about school experiences, reactions to other children (including the dawning of a special attraction to boys), and her sympathies for poor people. The diary reveals many thoughts and feelings that will still concern Nin in the published **Diary (Vols. 1 - VI).** The following excerpt shows her love for quiet, beautiful objects, her admiration for the strong, heroic type of woman, the agonizing isolation of self-doubt, and her dislike of aspects of urban America. Even as a young girl, she resorted to writing as the way to assert herself honestly.

> **I work hard at school but that does not prevent me**
> **from doing what I prefer to do. I have written a**

story *Poor Little One.* I only love either gay or very
sad things. Now I hate school, and everything American.
Mother asked me why. Why? Why? Because I love
silence and here it is always noisy, because everything
here is somber, shut in, severe, and I love gay landscapes, I love to see the sky, I love to admire the
beauty of nature, and here the houses are so tall, so
tall, that one does not see anything, and if you do
catch a little corner of the sky it is neither blue nor
pink nor quite white, no, it is a black sky, heavy,
lugubrious, soiled and blackened by the pride and
vanity of modern men and women. I say this because
I hate the modern. I would have loved to live in the
first century, in Ancient Rome, I would have loved
to live in the time of great castles and gracious ladies,
I would have loved the time of Charlotte Corday when
each woman could become a heroine. I must recognize
that I am crazy, but since my diary is destined to be
the diary of a mad woman, I cannot write reasonable
things in it! And they would not be my thoughts.

Anais was already impressed by dreams and had a prophetic
one.

. . . But I must tell about a rather singular dream I
had last night. First of all I found myself in a grand
salon carpeted in dark grey. I still remember how it
looked, but that is not interesting. I was seated on a
small wooden chair which smelled of pine. Then a
fine lady dressed in black velvet and wearing a belt
of diamonds or something sparkling, who first rushed
towards a grand piano on which she played, a long
and sad melody which made me sad. When she stopped
she went to a big easel, took a paint brush and began
to paint a very somber wood, with a pale blue sky in
the distance, she did that softly, and in one minute
she was through, then she advanced towards a big desk
and taking a pen and a big book, her big blue eyes
looking at me first of all, then at the sky, she began
to write pages and pages. I could see they were big
and beautiful poems full of charm, tenderness and

sweetness. I could not read them but I feel sure they
were beautiful. Then she closed the book softly, lay
down the pen, and came silently towards me and
then I heard these words: Choose. Oh, how much I
hesitated, first I remembered the beautiful melody,
then I suddenly turned towards the easel, it was so
beautiful, and with a paint brush I could describe the
sweet and charming landscapes, all the beauty of
nature. But suddenly, I turned towards the big desk
loaded with books, an invisible force led me towards
that corner, involuntarily I seized the pen, then the
lady smiling came up to me and gave me a big book
saying: Write, I will guide you. Without any difficulty
I wrote things which I think were beautiful because
the lady said to me pointing to a corner where men
with venerable beards, as well as queens and pretty
ladies were writing without stopping: Your place is
there. As soon as the lady was gone I softly dropped
the book, and I went towards the piano, I wanted to
try, first of all my fingers went very well, I like what
I was playing but suddenly I had to stop. I did not
know anymore. Then looking at the piano sadly I
thought: I cannot. Then I tried to paint, my land-
scape was already pretty but then I stop and see that
big smudges spoiled the whole thing, and then I said:
Adieu, I don't want this. Then I took up the pen
again and I began to write without stopping. My
dream was very long, but seemed so singular that I
wanted to tell it so as to be able to reread it.

Yet she reveals a profound ambivalence about the possibility of
communicating with others.

When I reread these pages I like to be able to say:
this is a special story. Does it matter if no one under-
stands? Am I writing for the world? No. My language
is unknown. What a joy it will be if I am overlooked;
my treasures will then belong to me alone. When I die
I will burn these pages and my thoughts scribbled here
will live only in eternity with the one who expressed
them.

Of course, if someone should understand, if someone should hear this contradictory language, these novel impressions, I would be very happy.

In her teens Anais Nin worked as a model for artists, which appealed to her dramatic, flamboyant side as well as gave her the opportunity to know other artists with whom she always felt an affinity. She also lived for a time with relatives in Havana, and became acquainted with another form of society. Nin's first novel, written when she was 19, contains material from these two episodes. This interesting novel is about a girl named Aline who poses for artists in order to earn money for her father and brother. Here is a page from it:

They set to work again, and while Zanelli mixed more paint he told Aline: "I'm surprised that your father lets you pose. Parents usually make a fuss over that."

"Oh, father did, of course, but what other work could I do?"

"You were born to pose for artists," Zanelli said emphatically. "You stick to that as a profession, and I prophesize that in a year David Sterling himself will have painted you."

"Who is David Sterling?"

"A painter who's been doing fancy things — you know the sort — paints clouds and fairies, etc., and he's always saying he hasn't found a woman he has wished to paint yet — they don't please him. Years ago we all enjoyed sending him the girls who came to our studios looking for work, and they all wasted their carfare, the poor things."

"Oh, how interesting," Aline exclaimed, slowly losing her first shyness. "He and my father would certainly agree if they met. My father says he will never write about women again, though he used to write novels about them once. He says that no woman ever comes up to a man's ideal. He's kept me home all these years, fearing I'd become like the rest of them, and hoping I might be saved by his constant teaching."

> **"And what on earth did he give you to amuse yourself with?" Zanelli questioned with apparent concern.**
>
> **"Books of poetry instead of dolls," Aline laughed, "And now I feel like taking a good look at the world outside."**

Aline conquers the awesome Sterling but in doing so discovers the importance of her work, and the story ends with her marriage to Sterling at the same time as she begins to write a book. A major theme of the novel is Aline's concern with being a *mere woman.* It seems as if only men are destined for success and freedom. Yet as a woman, she senses an enormous power. She desires to create and live boldly. She can be light and love dancing like other women but she is also solemn and thoughtful, qualities which she feels are not accepted in a woman by those around her. She sees that people have great capacity to hurt others as well as make them happy and she desires to express what she has observed in her writing. She justifies her obsessive interest in people's personalities by making it for literary purposes. Writing for her is the way she will heal the thousands of *thoughtless, intangible cruelties* people inflict on one another.

This 200-page novel is written in traditional third-person narrative structure. Occasionally a scene is prefaced by a quote, such as **As to us — we are uncertain people, who are chased by the spirits of our destiny from purpose to purpose, like clouds by the wind. — Shelley.** Someone who has written in the margins of this manuscript advised Nin to use her own lines to head chapters and to concern herself with plot construction. But Nin, the budding writer, is already writing what engages her rather than following how-to-write formulas. She expressed the feelings of Aline, although not as extensively as characters are portrayed in her later work. In this novel and her next one the story is advanced through dialogue far more than in Nin's later work.

Nin's next novel, written when she was 25, is labelled *unfinished* and is about 150 pages long. Like the first, it concerns a woman in relation to men artists. In this one the woman, Rita, is a muse of the men but a strong believer in the talents of women. The men are rather chauvinistic, at first thinking it is only their place to create, but by the end they learn to be more sensitive to Rita. Rita says:

"Poor Joseph! You have grown thin. You need me
to take care of you."

"Oh, not like before. I want other things now. I
think I understand what you needed. Now I would
like to know your thoughts, to let you live as I
live, with the things you love."

"Oh, let's not think about all that. I don't ever
want to write again. I'll just be your wife, and
nothing else."

"No, No, I tell you I know what it is you want.
I'll try and make you happier."

And then the calm, full days began just as before.
Joseph at the piano, Rita everywhere in the studio.
With this difference, that Joseph made constant
efforts to talk to her as he talked to his men
friends — seemingly considering her opinions. Rita
teased him about it but accepted it.

Her husband Joseph says:

"I can't say I find our marriage as peaceful or as
secure as before. You have shown a spirit which
frightens me, in a way. I suppose now it is up to
me to keep you from wanting to go."

Nin described this novel as written in imitation of D.H. Lawrence,
an author who profoundly affected her. Although this novel dissatisfied her, writing it gave her a firmer stance as a writer. In a
sense the influence of another author plays a role in helping the
young author achieve her own style, which Nin proved, for instance,
when she came to write the book about D.H. Lawrence. Another
significant influence in her growth as a writer, Nin felt, was her
knowledge of three different cultures and languages. She absorbed
the essences of French, English and Spanish even though she wrote
largely in English. According to Nin, she received from her Spanish
background — asceticism, fervor, physical and mental passion, **the
color and vividness that dramatizes everything,** the fusion of body
and mind, love for beauty and gesture, comedy and tragedy; from
the English — critical tools, analysis, lucidity, awareness of the
senses and subjection to them, the separation of body from head
with the emphasis on keen, selective thinking and discipline of the
body-machine; and from the French — a soft, misty quality, not

treacherously musical nor irrevocably clear but poised somewhere between, and tasteful selectivity, a resistance to impulse, deliberate transfiguration. She adds in her note, **The Spanish people live for an idea, the English die for an idea, and the French fight for it.** I imagine that Nin would do all three.

Nin's third unpublished novel, referred to as the *John novel* (although in early drafts the character later to be named John is called Duncan), is approximately 170 pages long. It was written when she was 26 years old and living in France again, occasionally dancing under a Spanish name. In this work Nin significantly progressed as a novelist. The reflective passages are longer, as though Nin is groping for the words that would precisely dramatize all the feelings. She demonstrates the ability to handle more deeply emotional material. In her efforts, some of the drafts are written on pages torn from calendar books, hotel stationery, small scraps, upon which she wrote whenever and wherever material felt alive to her.

Unlike the first novel, this one is divided into sections that are prefaced by Nin's own lines, as follows:

SHE SAW A VERY WIDE CIRCLE BEING TRACED AROUND HER. IT WAS MADE OF FLAMES. ITS CIRCUITOUS ROUTE HAD ENCOMPASSED TWO MEN WITH HER. SHE WAS IMPRISONED.

The leading character of this novel, written in the first person, is a woman who paints. She is married to Duncan, whose business is the Rubber Company and whose artistic production has been one book. Duncan talks about when he will create but cannot match the constant creative force of his wife. She is impatient with his passivity, and he cannot understand her intensity. She has met another man, a playwright named Alain who has the color and strong opinion that she missed in Duncan, and for whom she has a burning desire. She and Duncan have been married seven years though, and she regards her love for him as like a religion. **Their idea was that the test of a great love was endurance. Their love was a third truth, and their selves must revolve around it, must submit to it.** She does not want to hurt him. But she would reflect:

Yet she would have wanted one life, just one life with Alain. Why did she remember at this moment just one thing: no words, no embraces, no exaltation,

> just a twist of Alain's mouth, a voracious animal
> twist which had drawn the whole tidal rush of her
> blood to him? . . . She was afraid of her body.
> When she looked at it in the mirror she observed
> the mystery of its separate individual life. The silent
> curves contained emotions and pains, independent,
> secret, which she could not fully realize. In the
> mirror it was smooth; its movements were slow and
> supple. Inside, something was happening. She could
> feel· it when she heard music — then something
> stirred, very heavily. She was bearing two lives, two
> desires, two wills. The other was a menace because
> it was unknown, inaccessible.

The emotional tension of this novel is strong and taut; it moves more passionately than the first two. The woman faces imminent change in her life. She loves her work and exploration in living, as well as her husband. With her husband she has had a secure, comfortable, serene life, filled with qualities many people strive for. To change this life, possibly to leave it, requires courage of a kind that many people spend lifetimes avoiding. She must conquer enormous fears of the unknown. One of these is the guilt in realizing that she is smarter than her husband.

> The sudden realization that inevitably even if he
> gave all his life to literature she would outstrip
> him mentally gave her such despair that after
> talking very quietly and tenderly with him, hold-
> ing herself in, she slipped into bed and began to
> shiver and tremble violently, overtaken by a
> deathly feeling of cold, and then she felt she
> could not breathe anymore and she gasped and
> trembled like that for a few minutes while her
> poor darling called out to her and she could not
> answer.

Her love for Duncan becomes more painful because it is impossible to continue. She is dissatisfied with any lack of imagination in living. With Alain things are beautiful but she experiences increasing restlessness. She daringly criticizes his work, letting her intelligence

show. She sees limitations in men but does not want to destroy
them. She realizes that

> **. . . she lived now with all herself, this body so long
> ignored. She burned at last completely and living
> was revealed to her in a thousand ways. She melted
> into the world, into dreams, into flesh, into moist
> desires. Before she gave only the cold radiation of
> her thought — now she gave her burning flesh. She
> was woman.**

Significantly, the working title for part of this novel is *Woman
No Man Could Hold.* She will follow her mind, even if it takes her
away from any love. She dispels the illusion she built around Alain.

> **She had endowed him with the supreme poetical
> qualities, particularly of imagination. When she had
> discovered that he did not possess that why had
> she not ceased to be attracted? Because in Alain
> she had not been seeking the poet, but the big
> sensuous power and vitality. Her imagination was
> whipped and tormented by his literalness but her
> body had been enthralled, for all his matter of
> factness seemed a necessary part of real earth man.
> His earthiness answered a need in her. But if this
> were so how could she be cured without the
> physical experience? Because she had discovered in
> several ways that there was no sensuality in Alain,
> that it was all on the surface, in the eyes, voice,
> and body: there was vitality, intellectual force,
> vigor of speech, love of investigation, of oblique
> living, curiosity about everything but real sensuality.**

The woman wants to discuss Alain with Duncan but even
though they had **a capacity for intellectual tolerance they also
recognized in themselves a fund of emotionalism and a strong
wild jealousy.** Pity for him prevents her at first from speaking, yet
finally she does tell Duncan. Note how painstakingly the author
depicted this profound crisis between Duncan and his wife.

> **He had thought of her first, he had first given her
> pity and understanding. His love warmed her. But
> the pain was slowly awaking in his body; he
> suffered from a physical realization of the physical**

facts. It was this pain she had most dreaded. She
could do nothing for him. No amount of love could
heal him. Every time he looked at her body he
thought of Alain, and the thought and image were
intolerable to him. She would find him awake at
night, and know what he was thinking. It was his
turn to die, to be tormented by doubts and
jealousies, to touch the bottom of suffering. He
asked questions constantly. He was curious, fearful,
and though they let passion rush through them
often, and clung to each other, at moments he would
understand that the experience had enriched their
love, at other moments he questioned what had become of their love, whether she had ever hated him,
whether she had ever loved Alain more than himself.
She repeated that she had not loved him, that it had
been a physical bond. He had a terrible desire to know,
he had to know every detail of the scene. With Duncan's
head on her breast, she had to tell him, through tears,
every detail, and it was then she realized fully that
what she had thought a peak moment had become for
her an hour to loathe because the suffering in telling
him was far keener than any pleasure she had known
in obeying the impulse. This was true intensity, this was
the peak, the explosion, through suffering, of such
passion between her and Duncan as she had never
before conceived or experienced. The full, blinding,
startling realization of the preciousness to her, of
the inseparableness of their two bodies. Every
moment, in every embrace she could feel the
breaking forth of his love, never so violently expressed . . . it was absolutely new.

A few years later when Henry Miller read this novel, he wrote
in the margin: **This is rot! Too goddamned good to be true.** Miller
probably thought it was impossible for a woman to have the feelings
for her husband as Nin had portrayed them. But experience in the
life of women has shown that what Nin revealed is valid. More than
that, Nin has put into words the pain of such a situation and she
has shown a character who has sympathy for her husband and her

lover. The woman is not just selfishly seeking her own gratification nor bringing her relationship with her husband to a jarring conclusion, leaving both of them in despair from the sudden break. No, she has stayed close to the woman's feelings of love for her husband as a person, and in the end wins support from him in the form of belief and faith in her being. And similarly, the lover turns out not to be the goal either, as has been seen. Miller, who had a tendency to pay scant attention to the feelings of others in relationships, probably could not fathom this.

The next heading reads:

SHE HAD WANTED TO RETURN TO THE FIRST HUMAN CIRCLE. BUT IT WAS SMALL AND CONTAINED NEITHER MAN. SHE WAS ALONE IN IT. IN DESPAIR SHE LEAPED OUT OF IT AND BEYOND THE SECOND. THE THIRD CIRCLE WAS MADE OF PURE RADIANCE. IT DID NOT BOUND HER OR ENCOMPASS OR LIMIT HER. SHE COULD BREATHE FREELY.

The experience of writing this novel gave Nin a new perception of life that answered her childhood question — is life just a sad reality? Her awareness, which includes pride in herself as a woman and her ability to create, is both psychologically and philosophically perceptive.

> **. . . all the while she knew she was not running away from one man to another but from one feeling to another. The first was worth staying with, and undeserving of pain, and the second was, ultimately, hardly different. But living with the first was death, and going to the second was life. There was livingness even in the effort made to break the tension, to draw away, in the feeling of running to new sensations. All beginning was a kind of living, all settlement was a kind of death. The first man may not be different from the second, but the second could create a feeling. She was running imperatively towards life, she was running away from no one but herself, herself unresponsive to one man, responsive to another, that was all.**

**And the tragedy was that the men thought it was
they; the one who was left was hurt in his pride
and in his manhood, the one who was to receive
her was exulting in his triumph; there was no
triumph and no abandon, just the mere movement of life itself, of feelings that moved like a
river, that was all. There were no persons, no
real persons, and there should be no tears. But
the body of the woman who was growing thus
kept both men from seeing the idea, an idea for
which, if they had seen it, they would have had
no sympathy and no compassion.**

The process of life is like a continuous gnawing of the brain
on the nervous system. When the death of a relationship occurs, it
is felt in the psyche first and outward events follow afterward.
Death is withdrawal of energy from a person or work or place or
object and is experienced as pain. So, in this novel Nin has chroni-
cled death in a relationship and followed it further than she had
ever gone before; and in so doing she came upon spiritual truth.

In a fragment Nin noted that it seemed as if **her blood
eventually turned to ink. It was very economical.** Her sardonic
humor about herself shows how united writing and living have
become for her. Such explicit spontaneity could only come from
the labors of a desperately committed writer.

Actually in much of Nin's writing there runs a vein of ironic
humor that has gone unmentioned by critics. For her irony feels as
if her intellect opens a window and lets out fresh air. Humor can
be seen in a number of the stories Nin wrote in her twenties, of
which approximately 16 of the Northwestern Collection have not
been published. For instance, in a story titled *Alchemy,* a wife
receives visitors who have come to see her husband, *the great writer.*
The visitors ask to see *him* but *he* cannot be seen. The visitors
recognize details from the house and the wife's anecdotes, as having
appeared in the *great writer's* novels. As the wife patiently explains
his sources of characters and ideas, the visitors cannot believe the
great writer's ordinary wife could be the phosphorescent creature
he described in his books. The truth is that her life, her character
and friends, all her activities are the *great writer's* material, which
he has alchemized, as F. Scott Fitzgerald did of his wife, Zelda;

indeed she could even be the *great writer* herself. Through irony this story makes a humorous point about the creative process and also releases some of Nin's anger at being used and ignored as a writer.

Another story, *SUR/Realism,* makes fun of the random disassociation of elements that so often appeared in the work of the Surrealists. In this story a man, his wife, and another woman are in a House of Surprises, presumably of the mind rather than an actual carnival. The wife spends time in a room with a crusading American, but she worries that her young friend, who is afraid of men, is lost with her husband. She finally finds them; the woman is squealing delightedly and her husband observes dryly, **She had a very nice sweater on.**

In a story called *A Dangerous Perfume,* Nin's sardonic humor points up a landlady's repressive, puritanical, and dull stance toward life. Lyndall, a beautiful woman anxious to enjoy a balmy day in Paris, must see her landlady about the apartment she'd been living in. The landlady detects the aura of an exotic perfume, which upsets her. She hates it and wants to condemn the apartment. Lyndall is annoyed with the landlady's values, clearly aware that it is her love of beauty and passion that so offends her. She induces the landlady to admit her jealousy, after which Lyndall feels *she* could never live in the apartment again.

Other stories by Nin in the Northwestern Collection are fascinating dramatizations of states of feeling, written to more serious, symbolic purpose. Nin occasionally signed the name *Melisandra* to them. Most are intact and polished, while others are handwritten first drafts. They concern women, love, the chaos of inner struggle, the quality of life in today's society. An example is *A Spoiled Party* in which a strange woman enters a party unannounced and bewilders the guests. She is dressed in emerald green silk and has very large, turquoise eyes and sienna hair which stands out around her head airily. She will not speak, only looks into people's hearts and minds knowingly. She is the personification of self-knowledge.

In another story red roses are made the image of the terrible joy of fulfilled desire:

> **The red roses are flames, addressed to the flame in
> her. She cannot place them in a vase. She is over-
> flowing with their redness . . . They will burn the
> house, melt the snow, and burn her and all her**

**brothers and sisters, her mother, her father, the
neighbors. They will burn the village, and spread
in circles throughout the whole land and scar the
city.**

More so than in the novels the women characters of the stories
recognize the importance of work to their lives and are not content
with just the security offered by a man. In a story called *The Waste
of Timelessness* a woman is tired of the usual party and people and
wants explorations. She gets into a metaphorical boat and sails
magnificently away:

**Along the shore she saw her husband one day. He
signalled to her: "When are you coming home?"
"What are you doing this evening?" she asked.
"Having dinner with the Parkeses."
"That is not a destination," said she.
"What *are* you headed for?" he shouted.
"Something big," she answered, drifting away.**

Nin always had an intuitive grasp of the unexpressed feelings in
men and women. From childhood as we have seen she had an unusual
longing not to hurt others. This sensitivity plus her author's intelligence consistently gave her writing a compelling compassion. Because
as an author she conducted an honest struggle with the problems she
set herself in portraying life for the reader, she produced a quality
of livingness in her prose that made her material seem highly relevant.
Transmuting ordinary experience was the underlying purpose of her
writing in the novels and stories. In drafts of **House of Incest** she
will bring her life/material to a new level of awareness.

By the time Nin was 28 years old, which is when **Volume I** of
her **Diary** opens, her literary production had increased. She continued
to write stories, in addition to material that became parts of **Winter
of Artifice, Ladders to Fire,** and **House of Incest.** In 16 days
she wrote the critical book, **D.H. Lawrence: An Unprofessional
Study.** As **Volume I** of the **Diary** reveals this was a time of many
changes in Nin's life too. She both regretfully and joyfully was
leaving behind a certain life-style and opening herself to new relationships and experiences. The publication of **D.H. Lawrence** brings her
the literary friends that she always wanted. It seems as if the
emotional turmoil of the author's growth was the fuel generating
her prolific literary production at this time. In her case at least it

seems that the period of greatest suffering provided her with the themes of her best, most important works.

Because D.H. Lawrence's books helped shape Nin's own theories about literature and the relationships of men and women, she wrote the book about his work out of gratitude. Lawrence was a pioneer in expressing the psychological entanglements between mother and son, man and woman; being a man, he did not give as much attention to the relationships of father/daughter, which Nin eventually would do, or mother/daughter. Lawrence wrote about many of the inner effects of sex and the **blood of marriage.** He said that human love was relative and not an absolute, that at times individuals had to react away from one another in order to preserve their integrity. Marriage, he believed, was based on the pair's bond in one area and unknowingness in others. It was important to meet resistances in each other. Lawrence also wrote that the secret to **unutterable living** is obedience to the urges that arise in the soul, that these urges lead to new gestures, new embraces, new emotions, new combinations, new creations. In his work he took readers on his own soul-searching explorations, rather than merely entertain them. For him, writing was the profession of knowing the feelings inside a person and making new feelings conscious.

Nin pursued the same goal, which can be seen in the early novels and stories. She searched for the unconscious motivations behind people's actions, appreciated the life-giving power of sensuality and the necessity for creation and building one's own world. Lawrence had more empathy than most authors for the nature of woman, but he, like Freud and in a different way Jung, fell short in not being able to understand the woman seeking achievement in the world; they too often confused natural activity with aggression and gave it an exclusively masculine connotation. During this literary period, Nin began working with psychoanalyst Dr. Allendy, and her technical knowledge of psychoanalysis increased her capacity to understand the realm of feeling and psychic energy in human existence. Eventually through her work Nin would define in her way the psychological reality of the woman who builds and constructs other things besides relationships.

When Nin was 29 years old, **D.H. Lawrence: An Unprofessional Study** was published and among those who admired it was Henry Miller. He must have seemed to be a man incarnating D.H. Lawrence's ideas in the flesh. He was exuberant, warm, a great conversationalist. He too was finding his voice as a writer, was yet unknown, and totally devoted to writing. He had an extensive familiarity with people who knew poverty, slums, violence, lust, things which in human affairs are the other face of ideals, beauty and virtue. They shared revolutionary objectives in writing and had many conversations to refine them. Regarding Miller's writing, Nin is **baffled by his strange mixture of worship of life, enthusiasm, passionate interest in everything, energy, exuberance, laughter and sudden destructive storms. He uses the first person, real names; he repudiates order and form and fiction itself. Miller extols her matter, content, and vitality.** Both are inspired by André Breton's urging to write as one thinks, in the order and disorder in which one feels and thinks, to follow sensations and absurd correlations of events and images, to trust to the new realms they lead one into.

They inundated each other with their own work and works of others whom they admired; they revelled in each other's growth. Their rapport was intense; as they worked, they served as muse and sympathetic listener for each other. Nin wrote,

> **I have given him depth, and he gives me concreteness. . . I am merciless on his childish rantings . . . I only act as an analyst, helping him discover himself, revealing to him only his own nature, desires, aspirations . . . He helps me by always asking me to say more, to write more assertively, to clarify, expand, to be strong.**

Reacting to Miller's ideas about writing forced Nin to explain her own more fully. He was a merciless critic, as enthusiastic and exaggerated as he was in his own writing, and for Nin to survive that, without being destroyed, strengthened her. His notations in the margins of her manuscripts contain advice to learn new words, to cure herself of abominable locutions, and lively expansions of his own ideas (which *her* words stimulated). This relationship enabled both to more clearly see their own directions as writers. And that is the rare reward in the relationship between two people who write. Nin saw Miller lose sight of individual truth for intellectual world theories; whereas, she pursued the path of reaching for universal meaning within the individual. Eventually she withdrew herself from deep immersion in him. She felt that **The exaggerations he brings to his euphoric adventures in life, sex, food, laughter are wonderful. The inflation, bloatedness, giganticism he brings to his ideas, I suspect conceal a lack of focus and true insight.** Nin's future books could not help but benefit from such a literary encounter.

Besides leaving life in a Paris suburb for a vagabond world of artists, Nin was entranced by Henry Miller's wife, June. June was the fiery, beautiful, self-defined woman that Nin wanted fervently to be like at this time. This relationship is described in **Volume I** of the **Diary.** Nin's fascination with the personality of June leads her to explore this woman's nature artistically in the character of Sabina in **House of Incest.** Nin began writing drafts for **House of Incest** at this time. Into it, Nin put her ideas distilled from contemplating her life in her journals. She observed that because she lived life so intensely, she found herself in an abyss, a void, in which she must write books to get out. **She would be urged to create her own questions, her own world, her own characters — her own fulfillment. Because she could not bear the void, she would create a vast edifice.**

House of Incest is the last work of Nin to be considered in this study of Nin's early writing. It is especially interesting because the early drafts, contained in the collection at Northwestern University, include excised passages, and unpublished treatments that enlarge the meaning of this difficult, abstract work. Because **House of Incest** is a published work, the early drafts can be compared with the final form. The work is generally called a prose poem, because it is written in prose form but with narration more akin to poetry. But who really can tell where prose ends and poetry begins? Nin and poets gather at the same river.

From the outset this book, **House of Incest,** is structurally and emotionally different from all previous work. It is composed in seven psychologically sequential sections. It is narrated in the first person in terse, concentrated lines, making feverish paragraphs. Isolated lines in capital letters appear like warnings from the deep. Each individual presented reaches archetypal dimensions. It is as though all the early influences and practice have prepared Nin for producing this particular work. Nin's voice comes through, painfully direct, alarmingly fragile, yet extremely durable. It is as though the writer is in labor, giving birth to herself. A line emblazons the opening page; it could be the mantra for all of Nin's writing. **ALL THAT I KNOW IS CONTAINED IN THIS BOOK WRITTEN WITHOUT WITNESS, AN EDIFICE WITHOUT DIMENSIONS, A CITY HANGING IN THE SKY.**

In a note written while working on this book Nin wrote:

> **I am guessing at something so fantastic that I write like a medium. Voila le diable! A superstitious terror of life's madnesses and incongruities. The writer's divinatory power which surpasses her own intelligence . . . And to walk into chaos with a passion for crystallization does not imply to dispel the chaos. It means to discover more and more chaos, to descend further, to discover one cave underneath another, to become aware of the impossibility to seize.**

The more she wrote the more she discovered **unquenchable desire.** Following the images of the unconscious for her was a voyage that would open new pathways to life that fear had so far cut off. She desired easy flow between conscious acts and unconscious forces, harmony between the dark and light sides of the soul.

Like many others, including Henry Miller, I didn't understand **House of Incest** the first time I read it. Reading the words took me into such strange territory that I feared the lack of stability. Later, from reading the early versions of **House of Incest,** and getting a sense of how it developed, I came to appreciate it more and more. Reading it requires the maturity of experiencing confrontations of the self. I believe that with this book Nin reached the peak of her ability thus far. She proved herself capable to embark alone on a voyage into hell, like the mythical hero who must undergo terrible challenges in order to come back and save the people. She returns, battered, bruised, burned, but having learned the way of wholeness, healing, of centering the ever-gyrating soul.

House of Incest begins with a terrible beauty;

> **The morning I got up to begin this book I coughed. Something was coming out of my throat: it was strangling me. I broke the thread which held it and yanked it out. I went back to bed and said: I have just spat out my heart.**

There is an instrument called the quena made of
human bones. It owes its origin to the worship of
an Indian for his mistress. When she died he made
a flute out of her bones. The quena has a more
penetrating, more haunting sound than the ordinary
flute.

Those who write know the process. I thought of it
as I was spitting out my heart.

Only I do not wait for my love to die.

Thus the reader, by means of opening myth, symbol, and
tonality, enters a world of pain, where reason has failed and confusing images abound; it is a world of chaos and nightmare and
hopelessness.

As the book opens, the reader is taken to a state of unknowing
preconsciousness . . . or, the geological depth of the psyche. Rather
than an escape hatch, this is an inner place before the formation of
ego, where the source of self can be hunted down. Using a pre-
birth imagery the unpublished early version explains:

There was an Atlantide country sunk under the sea,
a race of men and women born under water, whose
first vision of earth and people was water stained
and veiled. This race of men and women spread
later over the earth, with water heaved eyes. Their
eyes were the color of water. There was to them,
at night, a kind of sulphurous transparency, and it
always seemed as if their bodies floated, as if the
flesh and bones were not brittle but made of rubber.
They swayed on their feet, the feet as light and
boneless as the feet of dancers. They stood on boneless toes, listening for ever distant sounds. The bells
of the Atlantide, with their faint, water covered
tones, which they feared not to hear in the zinc-
voiced earth city, among zinc-voiced men. They
were always listening for certain sounds, and
searching for certain colors. When you put them in
a water green room, where there were plants, or
perhaps gold fishes, or cactus, or perhaps many
water filled bottles, they stood at the threshold like

> a man troubled with a memory and then they swam
> into the room. They walked with a swimming stride.
> They seemed to cut through the air with a wide
> slicing of fins, they seemed to sense a direction which
> took no account of walls.

In the published edition the opening passage refers to the *uncompleted self* which is the basic thread to be followed in this work.

> My first vision of earth was water veiled. I am of
> the race of men and women who see all things
> through this curtain of sea, and my eyes are the
> color of water.
>
> I looked with chameleon eyes upon the changing
> face of the world, looked with anonymous vision
> upon my uncompleted self.
>
> I remember my first birth in water.

By the time we have read the first three pages of this book, we are aware of a new element in Nin's writing, the ability to create metaphors for complex inner realms. The reader has been carried off to the sea of primeval origins, beyond mere fantasy. Here exist effortless communication, natural movement of the body, joy, a place where the fury of war could never reach. It is also without systems of thought and political organizations. No rigidities, no laws, only flow in the here and now. In early notes she wrote, **The pattern was more harmonious, when we did not know it.** This remark suggests the similarity between Eastern philosophy and her psychological insight.

From **House of Incest: This Atlantide could be found again only at night, by the route of the dream.** Through the dream state the author recovers the psychological environment before the pressures of socialization took over. And also through dream imagery she tries to understand her birth and the woman she is becoming. She allows herself to be penetrated by the unknown, to let the images flow from her without relinquishing her power as author to select. C. G. Jung's line, **Proceed from the dream outward,** was important to Anais Nin. Dreams are the bricks with which this invisible house of incest is built. At one point Nin considered calling this work so full of dreams, *Thousand and One Nights in Montparnasse.*

The first section of **House of Incest** ends with **I awoke at dawn, thrown up on a rock, the skeleton of a ship choked in its own sails.** The earlier draft reads: **I woke in the morning and felt with my hand the inflexibility of reality, its ponderousness. The dissolution and the luxury, the lavishness and dewiness of the dream thrown up at dawn on a rock like the skeleton of a ship choked on its own sails.** The earlier lines, though not as poetic, clarify the meaning of the powerful image of the shipwreck. The narrator is confused, for the present immobilized, by inner storms.

The second section begins with an image to introduce Sabina, **Sabina's face was suspended in the darkness of the garden. From the eyes a simoom wind shrivelled the leaves and turned the earth over; all things which had run a vertical course now turned in circles, round the face, around HER face.** Upon her is focused the narrator's energy; she is endowed with mythical and supernatural powers.

All persons, encountered by the central character, **I** of **House of Incest,** can be seen as representative of psychological states of being in relationships. In the fourth section another woman named Jeanne will be introduced. To begin to understand Jeanne and Sabina it is helpful to know Nin's plan as revealed in the unpublished drafts of this work. When this work was first composed there were three characters named Alraune —— Alraune I, II and III. Alraune comes from a legend upon which Dr. Otto Rank has commented in a preface he wrote to **House of Incest.** It begins:

> **The humanized version of this hero-motif is the belief that the sterile woman can become pregnant and have children by eating some such 'magical food-stuff which in tradition gave birth to the hero . . . In medieval times we encounter a strangely elaborated legend around the Mandragora plant the root of which was supposed to look like a tiny human being — almost like an embryo — and to utter baby-like shrieks when it was pulled out from the earth which was done under particular conditions on account of its magical qualities.'**

As the product of a hanged man's semen transplanted into a whore's uterus, Alraune is the symbol of the bad woman as conceived by bewitched man who felt threatened by sexual destruction. She is birth through inhuman hate, by separation, where the man does not exist as a father. His semen is instrumental and the woman becomes the symbol of crude sexuality.

Alraune was seen as a woman conceived in the poisonous womb of a whore from the seed of a man who was hung. In Nin's notes she compared Alraune to the **mandrake with fleshly roots, bearing a solitary flower in a purple bell-shaped corolla. Narcotic flesh. A stemless plant with thick roots and a pale purple flower that shrieks when it is touched.** Then she created three aspects of woman which are variations on the theme of sexual union between man and woman. Alraune I is earth-sensuality because she is conceived in a moment of bliss between a couple. Alraune II is stillborn, because the man, in conceiving her, became aware that he was dead and destroyed his joy. Being dead, Alraune II has only a face and no body. She pulls away from the earth, thirsting after idealism. Alraune III contains both I and II. She is the artist who creates herself by uniting both earthly sensuality and the force of idealism. She is the only one conceived artificially (by artifice, art). She is given just a short space to live — in her books.

The narrator of **House of Incest** is Alraune III, the artist who unites the two forces pulling in opposite directions represented by Alraune I and II. The artist also is the only one capable of articulating completely the inner drama of the other women. The artist is compelled to express the drama because she is emotionally identified with both women. In that sense they are aspects of her self. The emphasis of the book is on the central character's integration of the battling forces. Alraune I is named Sabina in the published book. Nin's images in portraying Sabina reveal the power of this woman:

> **Born with gold-red jungle eyes, eyes always burning, glowing, as from a cavern, from holes in the earth, from behind trees . . . snake, lizard, lizard basking with solitary motionless eyes all fire and gold, snake cold and slippery, coiling on its alert tongue of fire. Gold-red jungle eyes hissing fire. The last film of fire like the transparent curtain of death, the glaze of the idol that worships itself.**

> **Born with a friable smile layer after layer that converged pyramidally into a human web. The mineral, prismatic, metamorphic texture of it. A lapidary smile that congealed the warm blood into**

stone, into precious gems that cut the flesh. The
slow lapidescence of countless experiences, producing the human geology of the whore's gem-like
smile, the liquid, blood-red light of sard behind
which the flesh crumbles away, revealing the
sepultures of love.

Jeanne in the published work is Alraune II, the idealist. In
House of Incest she is thus introduced:

Dilated eyes, noble-raced profile, willful mouth.
Jeanne, all in fur, with fur eyelashes, walking
with head carried high, nose to the wind, eyes
on the stars, walking imperiously, dragging her
crippled leg. Her eyes higher than the human
level, her leg limping behind the tall body,
inert, like the chained ball of a prisoner.

Jeanne is *dead* from the neck down.

Her face on its stemlessness was thrust away
from possessing a body. The face, thrust away
from the earth tautly with a breaking of the
nerves on her neck. Ascension! Ascension! The
dream! Thirst! The dilated eyes of intoxication
with the firmament. Her hands knotted and
tortured like the sinews of ancient trees, at the
mockery of possessing a body.

She shrieked when she was touched. She shrieked
at night. The eyes of the virgin who was never
fecundated, the eyes of Beatrice, the heroines of
English sonnets, the eyes of Shelley, the eyes of
Melisande, of clouds.

House of Incest should be seen as the narrator's quest for an
acceptable way to live among human beings and perceive all the
realities and still maintain an integrated self. Nin explained her
intent much later in **Novel of the Future**.

Projection and identification are living ways of
experiencing the life of another . . . I saw in
June some freedom of action which I wanted
to have and, as a young woman, could only
achieve by identifying with it. In *House of Incest*

the poetic image of two aspects of woman was pursued and became the two faces, the night and day
faces, of woman, one all instinct, impulse, desire,
impetus without control, the other who had sought
control by awareness. The only danger, of course,
is that one strong personality can submerge the
other; one can feel the loss of himself in the other
(as frequently happens in love), but there is no
life without danger, and the *other* danger, the
danger of alienation (and through alienation, non-
love, or hatred, or destructiveness, dehumanization),
I consider far greater . . . In the case of proximity
where the danger of losing one's self occurs, the
psychological drama becomes one of disentangling
the confusions.

The point of this relentless, desperate quest Nin also explained
in **Novel of the Future, You cannot relate to others if you have no
self to begin with. In order to respond, to excite, to participate, to
love or serve or create or invent, there has to be a self to generate
such emotions.**

To continue with the adventure of the self, the narrator is in-
exorably drawn to Sabina. In the **Diary** June Miller gives Anais her
bracelet as a symbol of their friendship. As the friendship progresses,
however, June's instinctual behavior goes too far and becomes
degrading. When she is drunk, she vomits and leaves Anais to clean
up the mess. Her lies wreak havoc. She is endlessly at war with
herself and others. Nin sees that she has hidden herself so long she
no longer knows who she is. In Nin's early draft of **House of Incest,**
Alraune I exchanges bracelets with her to indicate their being lost
in each other; they are each other's prisoners. Nin wrote, **I bruised
myself against her madness.** And in the published **House of Incest**
the steel jewelry is transformed into a vivid metaphor for the hard-
ness of her madness.

The steel necklace on her throat flashed like summer
lightning and the sound of the steel was like the
clashing of swords . . . Le pas d'acier . . . The steel
of New York's skeleton buried in granite, buried
standing up. Le pas d'acier . . . notes hammered on
the steel-stringed guitars of the gypsies, on the steel

> **arms of chairs dulled with her breath; steel mail
> curtains falling like the flail of hail, steel bars and
> steel barrage cracking. Her necklace thrown around
> the world's neck, unmeltable. She carried it like a
> trophy wrung of groaning machinery, to match the
> inhuman rhythm of her march.**

Another example of the way Nin transposes the daily reality of the **Diary** to vivid emotional metaphor is the instance in the **Diary** when Anais walks with June along a leaf strewn path, while June weeps over the end of love. In **House of Incest** this becomes:

> **the leaf fall of her words, the stained glass hues of
> her moods, the rust of her voice, the smoke in her
> mouth, her breath on my vision like human breath
> blinding a mirror . . . One woman within another
> eternally, in a far-reaching procession, shattering my
> mind into fragments, into quarter tones which no
> orchestral baton can ever make whole again.**

This process of transmutation of the ordinary universalizes the humans caught in conflict. Nin's skills with language contribute to the process: e.g., **Watching my sybaritic walk, and I the sibilance of her tongue.** Sabina has an **ancient stare,** a **voice that traversed the centuries.** Their union is created by timeless words. **She was an idol in Byzance, an idol dancing with legs parted; and I wrote with pollen and honey. The soft secret yielding of woman I carved into men's brains with copper words; her image I tattooed in their eyes.** Through deep examination Nin learned the secrets of the individual and as artist rendered them, giving existence an epic quality. **To tattoo an image in their eyes** is the artist's way of instilling truth in people through the psyche.

In **House of Incest** the isolation and alienation of the neurotic caught in the web of dreams are revealed in the persistence of nightmarish images. **The record was scratched, the crooning broken. The pieces cut our feet.** The narrator urges Sabina to become her.

> **Silence the sensational course of your body and you
> will see in me, intact, your own fears, your own
> pities. You will see love which was excluded from
> the passions given you, and I will see the passions
> excluded from love . . . Cease for a moment your
> violent deviations . . . I will take them up.**

The narrator becomes **the other face of you.** In an unpublished
note Nin described it more fully:

> **For an hour you were me, that is the other half
> of yourself. What you broke, burnt, and tore is
> still in my hands. I am the keeper of fragile things
> and I have kept of you what is indissoluble.**

But the identification proves to be wrong.

> **I am still with the obstinacy of images, reflections
> in cracked mirrors . . . I see two women in me
> freakishly bound together, like circus twins. I see
> them tearing away from each other . . . The loved
> one's whitest flesh is what the broken glass will
> cut and the wheel crush. The long howls in the
> night are howls of death.**

She feels the insanity produced by the inner tendencies pulling
apart like roots tearing at each other to grow separately, and the
constant straining to achieve unity. Sabina or Alraune I, if followed,
leads the self into mad whoredom. Her way is degraded. She represents incest in that the women love themselves in each other. Jeanne
or Alraune II leads the self into sterile, lifeless unreality. She represents incest in her self-defeated love for her brother, or love based
on an ideal impossible to realize. She longs to find someone like
herself but has enormous fears of doing so for then her realm of
solitude, where she reigns supreme, would end.

The images of terror and desire swell in magnitude. The tone is
feverish. The narrator (Alraune III) pursues and examines every
gesture, word, feeling for meaning. She compares herself to fish,
swimming in the labyrinthian waters. The fish swimming upstream
and downstream is the Piscean symbol, Nin's astrological sign.
She identifies with the light, facile, effortless movement of the fish,
as well as the duality of its Piscean voyages between the world of
miserable degradation and ideals, between painful crashes and soaring
ascension. She writes of the duality, the swimming backward and
forward, **There is a fissure in my vision and madness will always
rush through.** It is this which she seeks to close.

In psychological terms the central character has not found the
way to balance herself between these polarities. In addition, she
feels a distance between **the crowd, between the others and me.**
Distance creates solitude. **I cannot be certain of any event or place,**

only of my solitude. She yearns for an honest relationship but she cannot tell the truth to people, because it destroys them. She is **wrapped in lies which do not penetrate my soul. The moment I step into the cavern of my lies I drop into darkness.** She yearns for a place where **light had a sound and sunlight was an orchestra.** Light in **House of Incest** is reality, compared to the darkness of insanity which is feared.

But first the narrator must go all the way into the house of incest with Jeanne. It is **the only house which was not included in the twelve houses of the zodiac.** This grim house is the psyche of the depressed neurotic where self-love exists in many forms. The rooms of the house are chained together by steps; **visitors** talk to one another through dark windows without seeing each other's faces, just as the neurotic cannot see another, only himself. The rooms are **filled with the rhythmic heaving of the sea.** Here is the neurotic's longed for hidden womb, where the fish are immobile, **glued to painted backgrounds.** Everything stands still in the house of incest because they feared that movement would cause love to flow away from them. Only the cold absence of pain exists in the frightening climate of neurosis. Fear of change locks the individual into this place of hibernation, solitude and distance from others.

She (Alraune III, *I*) sees examples of incestuous love. There is a painting of Lot with his hand upon his daughter's breast, showing joy and fear racking her body. The same feelings are seen between brother and sister, mother and son. She leaves Jeanne and walks **into my own book, seeking peace . . . As I move within my book I am cut by pointed glass and broken bottles in which there is still the odor of sperm and perfume . . . More pages added to the book but pages like a prisoner's walking back and forth over the space allotted to him.** Tortured by fear of madness and immobility she tries to unify the fragments of her self through writing, the art of forging a whole in creation. Still, there are no signs of rebirth, despite her efforts. **As artist I imagine that I created myself, and that it was I who tore myself out of earth and water, broke all shells, and looked with chameleon eyes upon the changing face of the world, looked with anonymous vision upon my completed self.** As artist, with the ability to create herself, she hoped to find the key to salvation.

But then she **walked out of my book into the paralytic's room.**
The paralytic sits before a notebook of blank pages, saying **I want
to tell the whole truth, but I cannot tell the whole truth because
then I would have to write four pages at once, like four long
columns simultaneously, four pages to the present one, and so I do
not write at all.** He represents the indecisiveness of the intellectual
analyzing world issues. Next, Sabina, Jeanne and **I meet the modern
Christ, who is crucified by his own nerves, for all our neurotic sins!**
He is based on the figure of Artaud as Nin perceived and identified
with him. He possesses the **language of nerves.** The modern Christ,
like Artaud, says he **was born without a skin.** He personifies the
person aware of everything so acutely that the agony is unbearable
and others isolate him from society, as for example in a mental
institution. The modern Christ wants to help the three women. **But,**
Nin writes, **none of us could bear to pass through the tunnel which
led from the house into the world on the other side of the walls
. . . where there was daylight and joy.** They feared to approach
reality, the light of day; they could not believe freedom was there.

In the earlier drafts of **House of Incest** the role of astrologer
took the place of the paralytic and the modern Christ. The astrologer,
familiar as he is with the houses of the zodiac, ancient metaphor for
the potentialities of people, is a kind of god-the-father figure. He
created the three women, and it is as if the women are confronting
their maker. He also is endowed by Nin with the characteristics of
the alchemist and the psyche-analyst who presumes to understand
everything. (Dr. Allendy, Nin's psychoanalyst, incidentally as the
Diary shows, was an astrologer and wrote about alchemy.) In Nin's
early draft this doctor is beseeched to close the **fissure in her
vision.** He dispenses compassion and clairvoyance. She writes: **He
leaned over my madness and I stood up without crutches.** He cures
her of lies, the need for them. The three Alraunes seduce him.
The astrologer's coat of armor breaks and falls. He is revealed to
have no sexual powers. And the narrator is left feeling that in man —
man as father, lover, doctor, teacher — she has no guide. She has
only guilt for having smashed his armor (broken his mask of theories
and ideologies) and exposed the absence of his presumed potency.
It is a powerful scene and in some ways stronger than the later
version.

In the **Diary** Anais Nin showed how men had failed her. In the portrait of Dr. Otto Rank, she wrote: **This is my fourth attempt at a truthful relationship; it failed with Henry because there is so much he did not understand; it failed with my father because he wants a world of illusion; it failed with Allendy because he lost his objectivity.** Furthermore, she was convinced that man-made knowledge and religious theories created guilts and distanced people from true aware- ness. In the final version of **House of Incest** the central character sees the uselessness of the paralytic, representing the controlled intellectual man, and the modern Christ, who in his extreme hyper- sensitivity is unable to communicate with most people. Somehow she will have to find her own way, not dependent on man. By now the reader recognizes the centrality of this issue in Nin's work. The conclusion of **House of Incest** resolves this in a large vision.

One of the features of Nin's work is that the reader must fully participate with the central character's explorations, never knowing what moment or what place will lead away from death to the moment of rebirth. The **not knowing** or the **cloud of unknowing** is essential to the harmony of psychological process. Knowingness or analysis retards the movement toward renewal. In **House of Incest** Nin has the image of a woman, without arms, dancing, appear before the characters, which is precisely the way psycho- logical process works. After all the stress in searching has gone as far as it is going to an image presents itself to the mind. And this image is endowed with an intense energy because it is the product of deep inner striving.

In the image a woman, dancing, listens to music they could not hear. Her arms

> **were taken away from me, she sang. I was punished for clinging . . . I clutched at the lovely moments of life . . . My arms were always tight and craving to embrace . . . And I strained and held so much that they broke. Everything eluded me then. I was condemned not to hold . . . I could not bear the passing of things. All flowing, all passing, all move- ment choked me with anguish . . . And she danced; she turned with the earth turning, like a disk, turning all faces to light and to darkness evenly, dancing toward daylight.**

The wisdom shown this woman is that she must not hold onto

experience or people she loves. She has to let them be. She has to allow emotion to go from pain to joy with acceptance. She has to understand that the changes of dream and involvement with the world and people, of love and hate, **are as permanent and cyclic as the earth turning on its axis.** This rhythm is spoken of in Eastern philosophy and depth psychology; it is described as centering, being here now, letting life flow through one without judgement, without seizing it in any attempt to impose order, as if one were transparent.

In Nin's first thoughts about this image, she wrote:

> **When I ran through the fields in the winter, I put my arms around the trees because they were sighing. When it was warm I flung my arms in the air to embrace the warm light. When I was joyous I danced with my arms and I awoke in the morn- ing with undulations of my arms, like incantations. I wanted to rock pain and caress and heal and surround and encompass. When people suffered I put my hand on their knees but also if they were full of life I tried to put my arm around their life. I was all a circle. I circled, I tried to close until I was punished.**

She learned not to hold, but to give with abandon, and to allow herself to be permeated by all feelings. The image of the woman who opens herself to give, without holding, is also a dancer. And dancing is the movement of a person in relation to life. The movement also suggests making art from life. It is done to music that is only heard to herself, which means that it comprises her unique growth, her own fears, laughter and breathing. It is the indiscernible unique destiny dwelling in all things. In the early version of this work, Nin summarized her ideas further in the unifi- cation of the Alraunes.

> **The idea is that Alraune III (woman-creator) swallows both I and II in meeting the paralytic and modern Christ (Artand) which represent neurotic love experience. In meeting of dancer and becoming of dancer Alraune III flows into pure movement again — something comparable to flow of birth — that is, because life, being neurotic love, being too difficult, she dances or**

**writes — movement glorified because it is impossible
to make movement of life equal to movement of
imagination. The failure of the life flow, making
creation flow.**

Thus, in **House of Incest** one significant result is the synthesis
of woman and artist. Art is the creative spirit's response to life.
The line between life and art is not clear, for Nin learned that
much of her understanding of life came through the contemplative
act of her writing. Sometimes it seemed as if the most intense
living took place in the writing — for example, when the power of
insight took over and washed away angry frustrations. Furthermore,
Nin perceived that life is not just a **sad reality** as she mused in the
childhood diary but life is the process of movement between joy
and pain. Life seen as movement from feeling to feeling, rather than
to other individuals, Nin discovered in writing the *John novel.* In
House of Incest the fluctuation is shown to be as much a law as
the cyclic turning of the earth between night and day. Life is not
free of opposites. There is no permanent euphoria, no everlasting
freedom, but there is movement and the opportunity for creation.

House of Incest is akin to the work of serious philosophical
and literary masters. Critics who are unfamiliar with psychological
cycles and symbolic gestures do not immediately comprehend Anais
Nin's far-reaching implications as a writer. Nin focused on the inner
adventures of the self and selected only germane, rather than mun-
dane details for use in her fiction. She is a psychological realist,
concerned with the forces that motivated people's actions. One of
her resources for **House of Incest** had been dreams. She did not
just piece dreams together, as on a chain, a method Henry Miller
used to lesser effect in **Black Spring** at the same time as Nin wrote
House of Incest. Missing in Miller's approach was the context of
events, pressures, and relationships. Nin knew that such imagery
meant nothing and had no emotional value when used alone. It
must be seen in context of the full human drama.

Nin's literary style evolved to suit her material. In **House of
Incest** can be seen a collage technique in the structuring of important segments. In a collage only the most vivid and outstanding
pieces are selected, shaped, and placed in juxtaposition with others
to build up a whole picture. The final image may be more or less
abstract; the only thing it does not employ is a continuous line,

just as Nin's work does not have a conventional plot line. This form Nin used in her later novels and it most successfully represents the interior happenings of the mind. Nin believed that writing should sing, shout, cry, laugh, make love, etc. Music, color, texture, sculpture have been sources of inspiration.

With the inherent rhythm and emotional quality in words Nin hoped to penetrate people's minds. By engaging their emotions she hoped to influence people. Thus, she explored and reproduced subtle shades of feeling, carried even to the utmost personal confusion. The significant breakthrough that **House of Incest** represented for Nin the writer is that she wrote it with her whole self. There is no holding back, only refinement for clarity and beauty. The feelings rush through her words, like the sound of water crashing over rocks.

If Nin's passion is contagious, then others will take responsibility for their lives and psyches. She hopes people will become less afraid to examine their personal imagery and large emotions. Nin believed that repression of the contents of the psyche was a major cause of society's ills, its international wars and destruction. As C.G. Jung said, the source of all the evil in the world is found in the human psyche. People present the greatest danger to the world and themselves. Nin felt that through writing she could express the **naked truth, which is unbearable to most, and overcome people's resistance to truth.** Her politics were to attack ugliness, cruelty, despair, anger at their psychological roots and supplant them with moral, physical, and aesthetic beauty. This urgent social desire animating Nin's writing is like a strong wind blowing through our modern crises.

It seems as though **House of Incest** stands at a pivotal point in Nin's literary career. Nothing else before or after it is quite like it; and writing it seems to have given Nin new confidence in the direction of her future work. In the seven novels that followed Nin presented the psychological struggles of other women in their relationships and life experience. Nin wrote in **Novel of the Future** that her later **novels were to be the constant description of going into life and back into the dream to seek the self when it lost its way. In a sense, I continued to say: the dream is the key, the source, the birthplace of our most authentic self.** This method and philosophy of Anais Nin are the treasures brought back from her **season in hell,** the writing of **House of Incest.** The wisdom and passion wrested from the experience of that book produced many flaming embers that burned for a long time afterward. There was so much that went beyond the scope of one book, so many aspects to explore and characters to create — Djuna, Sabina, Lillian, Stella, Jay. So many questions to pursue in quieter moments, when living permitted the possibility for more of the magic of writing.

Conclusion

In closing I offer the results of a continued contemplation on these three women, who have been wisdom figures for my life. Here symbolic imagination reveals the inner connection between me and the women.

Frances Steloff, Anais Nin, and Maria Montessori appear to me. They kneel on the ground, dressed in long, white tunics, which flutter in the summer breeze. Nearby is a large pond, around which are willow trees and tall marsh grasses. A sunflower arches its head, heavy with seed. I hear a tomato drop to the ground — splat. On the still, dark surface of the water lily pads float.

I feel a cooling mist on my face, as I approach the women. I see that in front of them a large circle has been drawn in the dust. The women chant, **Oh Valerie, Oh Valerie, Oh Valerie.** My very bones vibrate.

Oh Women, I say, **you are my mothers. I want to be as strong as you were in your lives.**

The women answer as one, **We are always here.**

I know. It is I who is not. But now we are together. Let us enjoy each other's company.

Anais Nin lies back and says, **I am happy. My lace skirts billow; the air is perfumed. My skin is soft as a peach, and my hair is braided with flowers. My lips caress the grass.**

Frances Steloff speaks, **And I am peaceful here, even though the world is full of conflict. But if I lie too long, I will not get up again.** She rises to sit on her heels. **I am an old prune now, but I have learned my lessons well. I speak what I think is right. Life is really simple. You must stick to what you love. That is the best way but it is also tough. Stay straight as an arrow. Simplify. Leave out of your life what doesn't matter. All I have to offer is my life, my past involvement with the Gotham. One's body is the substance.**

I respond poetically: **O Fire Within**
> **Flame of the womb is sexual passion**
> **Flame of the head is creativity**
> **Longing and desire**
> **The Body contains you, is the**
> **Shackle for good and evil**
> **No one knows how the flames lick me**
> **Burning for release**
> **Purify me!**
> **Forge a splendid shield.**

Nin says to me, **You have my blessing. I am with you. I take your hand as Virgil did Dante's. I am also Beatrice. I have united European values and American vitality. I have dug and excavated rare treasures, all of which I have shown you. Look hard. Observe well. Go carefully. Although it may take a long time, describe what you see. I will soon leave you and then you will have to dig, excavate, and lead others. Describe the flame within.**

Later Maria Montessori stands up, saying, **I am seized by such restlessness. I am afraid I can't lie still.** She rises in the air, her skirts a bulbous balloon. **I like this much better. I can see more from here. Down there I am too close to the ground.**

Oh Montessori, although I have never met you before in person, you have inspired almost every move I've made with my family.

You want to live with joy, like the children. They are by nature good and preserving and independent. Are you centered as they are? Do you follow your sensitive periods?

I try, but it is so hard.

Valerie, work through the imagination and life of others, as I do. The process is deep and difficult. You must be watchful, lest you lose your opportunity.

I am so happy just looking at all of you, being with you, my mothers.

The women as one, **You are your own mother, you know. You are your own mother. Look at your face. You looking at your face is your mother looking at you.**

But I have many fears. You are serene. I cannot be.

We are at the end of our lives and have survived many struggles and changes. You are just beginning.

May we kiss?

We kiss each other sweetly, softly on the cheeks, forehead, hair, then shoulders, hands, and lips. Our arms hold our bodies together lightly. We seem to entwine each other airily, full of delight and love. Then arise longing and desire for our whole beings to know the ecstasy of union, for all to merge and know one another, closely for now.

Enfolded a long time, the knowledge and qualities of our beings are blended and melted. We become liquid. Then we burst into fire. We are a tall, narrow flame, shaped like a tree, burning and crackling for centuries. We cry. Tears stream from our eyes, shrieks and moans from our mouths. At last the fire subsides and we are in a desert. Everything has turned to sand. We are the only four women in the world.

I feel like Dorothy of Oz or Alice in Wonderland, standing lost with my friends. We have become like children. Montessori sits down to ponder, while Steloff holds the hand of a trembling Nin. I wonder where we will eat, and think I know the way to a city. I lead us to a strange old village, where we find a restaurant. Inside the room is dark, although the walls are white and red geraniums are in the windows. Guitar music is played and a Spanish-Indian man serves us wine and salad. We joyously celebrate our safety.

While we eat, a crow flies in the window. It seems like an omen. I watch it fly out again toward some trees, which suddenly part to reveal a wide expanse of white sky. We are drawn up, as by a vacuum, and flown, quite exhilarated, back to the lush pond. The four of us sit in a circle, silently smiling at each other.

Sometime later I dip my hand in the water, feeling it trickle coolly over my skin. I am tempted to ease my naked body in and swim. The others watch me as I laugh and play in the water. Toward the center of the pond the ripples of the pond seem black. I stay away from the deep but am filled with dread. Near the shore I find an old log with soft bark to lean on. The air is calm. My breast seems very white. I cannot see my lower body beneath the surface of the murky water.

Lightning strikes me — through the bones. I am shattered; yet I feel the paralysis and terror. The sockets of my eyes look out in shock. My skin shrivels and slips into the water. It floats toward bramble bushes near the shore. There it is sheltered for millennia. Decomposed, it floats out on top of the water like salt.

The three women watch stone-faced. I hear the words: **Saline . . . saline . . . saline . . .** from which the future me will emerge.